HARDPRESS.NET
HOME OF HARD-TO-FIND BOOKS

Scenes and Thoughts
by Scenes

Copyright © 2019 by HardPress

Address:
HardPress
8345 NW 66TH ST #2561
MIAMI FL 33166-2626
USA
Email: info@hardpress.net

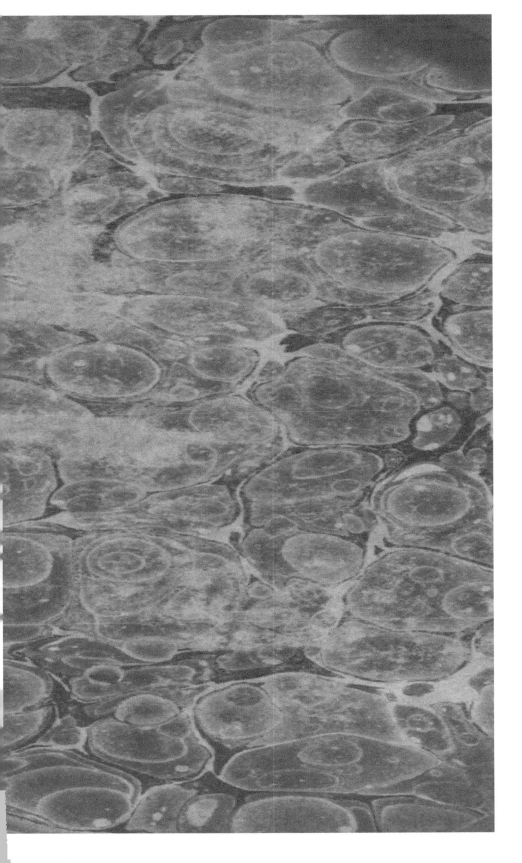

SCENES

AND

THOUGHTS.

SNATCH FROM OBLIVION EACH PASSING HOUR,
AND NOTE EACH RISING THOUGHT.

LONDON:
PRINTED FOR G. B. WHITTAKER, AVE-MARIA-LANE.

MDCCCXXIV.

50.

LONDON:
PRINTED BY WILLIAM CLOWES,
Northumberland-court.

CONTENTS.

		Page
WRITING A BOOK	. . . . .	1
RETROSPECTION	. . . . .	9
A " TALE OF LOVE"	. . . .	13
REFLECTIONS	. . . . .	96
FOND MEMORIALS	. . . .	106
BENEVOLENCE	. . . . .	118
HOME	. . . . .	136
A COUNTRY SUNDAY	. . . .	150
A MARKET-DAY	. . . . .	176
HUMBLE VIRTUE	. . . . .	203
FASHION	. . . . .	213
THE AFFLICTED FAMILY	. . . .	221
SCANDAL	. . . .	236
THE FAREWELL	. . . . .	249
THE POET'S HOUR	. . . . .	273

SCENES AND THOUGHTS.

WRITING A BOOK.

Answer this question, friend,—"I prithee why,
If all the world be mad, why may not I?"

I WAS one night sitting for an hour or two in my
little study, or *sanctum sanctorum*, by the side of
that cheering companion, a bright glowing fire.
I had laid down my book, and, throwing myself
back in my elbow-chair, with my head comfortably
resting upon one of my hands, I gave myself up
to meditation. To follow the mazy labyrinths of
thought through which I unconsciously strayed,
or to describe the excursive flights of my truant
fancy, would now be as impossible as it would be
useless; but I distinctly remember, that after
having for some time indulged in the most whim-
sical speculations on various subjects, the thread of
my ideas was suddenly and rudely broken by the
fall of my book, which, having laid open across my
knee, a slight movement of my foot tossed to the

B

ground; and, that when I had replaced it in its former station, their original current was completely changed, and they became employed in dwelling on the literary labours of man, and reflecting on the immensity of that intellectual store which past ages had successively hoarded together. I considered the invaluable mass of learning which had been collected by the mighty historians, philosophers, and orators of ancient Rome, and the inestimable treasures of taste and genius which have been handed down to us by the poets, the painters, and the sculptors, who flourished during the glorious era of Grecian freedom. I then, passing over in my mind's eye the period of gloomy inanity, or savage barbarism, which shed the darkness of night over a world so lately illumined by the brilliant rays of intellect, traced the revival of art, and science, and literature, from their first faint dawnings to that splendour with which they once more shone, till I found myself again in the nineteenth century, from which I had retrograded for a while, only finally to return to it again. And then I naturally began to consider how far my own age was distinguished by the efforts of literary genius, and what rank it would hold among the many which preceded it, in the estimation of those who were yet unborn. But alas! here I found hat I had embarked on a wide ocean to which I could see no bounds or limits. An endless expanse of *print* was before me, and I felt sure that one fleeting life would not traverse even a twentieth part of it. " All the labours of antiquity," thought I, " dwindle into nothing, compared with those of my contemporaries, for only a few of the most renowned sages, or the most approved scholars, dared *then* to attempt the instruction of mankind; but now, so much have the mental faculties strengthened and expanded, that thousands present continually to their fellow creatures some lettered proof of their perfection, without suffering a single twinge of compunction, or being compelled to struggle with the troublesome feelings of timidity or self-distrust." Here a sudden thought, the offspring of one of those involuntary impulses which sometimes impel to " deeds of valour and renown," led me to ask myself why, when such a multiplicity of volumes daily issue from the press, from the massy Encyclopedia down to the penny pamphlet, —when every body is writing for *print*, and every body is reading what is written, I, *even I*, should not also shew something from the stores which lay, for ought I know, rusting in my brain, to enrich the mighty stream? " Bless me!" I cried, starting with some vehemence from my reclining position, " I have lived all the days of my youth, nay, my sun has already passed its meridian, and not

single line have I ever composed for the good of
my fellow creatures.   Ingrate that I am ! to draw
so largely from the possessions of others, without
contributing a single mite towards the general fund .
But there is an old adage that tells us it is ' never
too late to mend,' so I will set about to make my
' amende honorable ' this very instant ;" and with
this praiseworthy resolution, I actually started up,
provided myself *instanter* with paper and ink, cut
into one of my best crow-quills, and sat down. in
due state to commence my important task.

But here an apparently insurmountable obstacle
presented itself.   Amidst all the abundance which
I had been considering,—in this great literary
harvest—what ear of wisdom remained for me to
pluck for the benefit of others?   Not one, alas !
was left untouched; and I knew too well that I
had not learning enough to display any considerable
portion of erudition in expatiating upon the dry husks
that were left, nor sufficient ingenuity to extract
from them any alluring sweets or wholesome nourishment.   This unforeseen difficulty threw a terrible damp upon my heroic resolves, and checked
all my ardent hopes; and I sat some time with my
pen idle in my hand, and looking, I dare say, the
image of that grim demon, Despair.   At last, a
new light darted upon my mind.   " If I cannot
expatiate upon any thing else," I exultingly ex-

claimed, " I can at any rate discuss myself.
Others, with the utmost complacency, have dwelt
upon their own exploits, and narrated their own
adventures, and why may I not profit by so excellent an example ?" No argument of any weight
occurred to me to oppose my inclination, and with
this wide and interesting field open to my view, I
no longer had to lament that I had nothing to say.
The only question that remained to be solved was,
at what point, in so extensive a region, I should
commence my undertaking ? Shall I, thought I,
indite a full and regular account of myself and my
affairs, beginning with my " birth, parentage, and
education," thus adhering to the excellent precept
of " doing every thing in order,"——or shall I rather
narrate merely such passages of my wondrous
career as shall best please me, interspersed with
some of the sublime collocations to which they have
given birth ? I at length, after all the deliberation
which so important a subject demanded, decided on
the latter; and having thus overcome all my difficulties, I once more replenished my pen, and actually
commenced the truly interesting lucubrations which
I now send forth to make their own way through
this perilous world, knowing too that they must
necessarily meet with the harsh tauntings of scorn,
and the mortifying glances of contempt, and fear-

another guise, is neglected on account of the plain-
ness of its appearance.   I would have taste refined,
but still natural; minute, but not fastidious.   I
would have it shrink from all that militates against
the purest virtue, and scrupulously nice in its sense
of its extent and its boundaries; but I would *not*
have it lose the reality in the shadow; I would *not*
have it deceived by the false glitter of smooth
words and flowing language.   I would have it
clearly discriminate between the intrinsic value of
the original gem, and the deceptions and highly
finished gloss of its counterfeit.

RETROSPECTION.

How sweet in Retrospection's page to trace
  Each pleasing scene to recollection dear;
Again to live in friendship's warm embrace,
  Again to bid each cherish'd form appear.

AMONG the numerous pleasures which a kind Providence has placed within our reach, none appears to me more sweet and soothing than that which is afforded by *Retrospection*, or the power which we possess of retracing past events, and living as it were again in scenes of lost delight, when joy shed its vivid rays upon the picture, and happiness encircled us with its bright but transient halo. Sometimes, indeed, it only presents us with a view of almost forgotten suffering, and brings to us the remembrance of sorrow, which, though calmed and softened by the healing hand of time, may be again partially ignited, like a half-smothered flame by the faithful torch of memory. But, besides that it is good for the mind to be thus recalled to a sense of its past afflictions, and reminded by powerful experience of the uncertainty and instability of all human joys and possessions, it frequently diffuses a solemn and melancholy satisfaction, which appears to me to be in truth and verity the real " luxury of woe." If those to whom we were once united by the closest bonds of love and sympathy, have been torn from us by the hand of unpitying death, and thus severed for ever from our mortal eyes, how delightful is it to be able to place their loved forms before the mental sight, as they once were, the living objects of our warmest affection. To call back every kind look, and hear again every expression of attachment and of tenderness. To feel in imagination the close embrace of unfading friendship, and listen to the warning accents of paternal solicitude or maternal anxiety. This is a bliss which more than overpays the pang with which truth destroys the blest illusion; and to enjoy which, I would endure all the agony with which its painful intelligence first seizes on the soul. Some, perhaps, may be disposed to blame the indulgence of such feelings, but, I repeat, that I think them productive of the best possible effects, by softening, but yet not weakening the mind, in rousing each sweetest feeling of our natures, and kindling in our breasts the noblest emotions of which they are susceptible.

I love also to review all those little incidents, of trifling importance indeed in themselves or their consequences, but which compose the great sum of human life, and which, although reduced into mere specks by the operation of time, yet appeared once as objects of no inconsiderable magnitude, and claimed a large portion of my thoughts and attention. I then recall the feelings which they excited,—the resolutions to which they gave birth,—and the ideas and actions which they prompted ;—and, comparing them with my present views of the same things and occurrences, smile at the changeability of the human heart, and the inconstancy of human opinion. This too is, I think, by no means, an useless or an idle speculation. It is one which tends greatly to enlarge our conceptions, and open to us an insight into the tempers and characters of men, and the means by which both are influenced or changed. It teaches, what otherwise can be learnt only by experience ; and, by showing what was censurable or praiseworthy in our past conduct, enables us more clearly and easily to discover what deserves commendation, and what calls for blame, in our present line of action. It is like a person, who, not content with viewing the exterior of a great and curious machine, examines minutely into its interior formation, and endeavours to penetrate the various springs and powers by which its different movements are effected.

As we cannot lay open therefore to inspection

the hearts of our fellow-creatures, we must be content to examine our own, and draw our conclusions not by their immediate feelings, but by those which are past; not only by the present actions which they impel, but by those also which they once caused, compared accurately and impartially with each other.

Retrospection has also another advantage attending on it,—I mean the constant amusement which it is capable of affording, and, therefore, the comparative independence which it causes, of other kinds of entertainment. Indeed, at times, when all else fails to interest, or to calm the mind, this faculty will, properly exercised, produce a most pleasing effect, and perhaps prove an effectual cordial. In fine, the past is like a landscape in nature, on which the eye can rest with security and certainty at least; and, although the gloomy cavern, and frightful precipice *do* obtrude themselves, the first may generally be finely contrasted with the smiling fertility of the scene which surrounds it; and the other makes us only doubly value the safety in which on the whole we have been preserved; while the present resembles a painting, whose colours change, or fade away, as we survey it; and through the dense mists which hover over the future, we attempt to penetrate in vain,

A " TALE OF LOVE."

Oh! sweet is that lovely spring-time of life,
 When Hope sheds its brilliant rays,
And illuming a region of sorrow and strife,
 All its fugitive beauties displays.

WHEN I was in the meridian of youth, that season
of life in which hope and expectation gild every
scene with their bright and vivid rays, I was suddenly seized with a violent fever, which threatened
to terminate my short but not unpleasing career;
and my anxious family long considered my condition as entirely hopeless. I, at length, however,
got the better of the disease, although the extreme
weakness to which it had reduced me, was almost
equally alarming. But even this, a naturally good
constitution, and the unremitting tenderness and
attention of the kind friends with whom a gracious
Providence had so amply blessed me, gradually
overcame, and I began to experience all those blissful feelings and emotions which only those can
taste who have for a time been deprived of that
invaluable gift, health. I never shall forget the

first day on which I was allowed to inhale the fresh breezes of a sweet summer's morning, and revel in the warmth of a bright summer's sun. I felt a heaven within my soul, and my eyes seemed to wander through the regions of paradise. All my suffering—all my confinement was forgotten ; and the pulse of joy, the throb of ardent gratitude alone filled my heart, or existed in my memory. The first transports of my happiness soon subsided, but a calm and placid enjoyment succeeded, and no period of my life recurs to my remembrance in which I experienced more complete happiness than that in which I was regaining a great portion of my former strength of body, and vivacity of mind. As the bloom of health did not however so speedily revisit my cheek as my tender parents desired, they proposed that I should go some little excursion, hoping that change of scene would complete my re-establishment. Many plans were accordingly agitated, and many projects formed by them, for best effecting this kind purpose, and, (as I afterwards understood,) while I was endeavouring to do justice in my own room to the good things which they sent to me every morning to tempt my fastidious palate, the breakfast table down stairs was the place at which all these various cogitations were assiduously pursued for my benefit. But I must offer to my reader a family picture which will

present to his eye these good and valuable relatives,
although I fear my pencil will fail in delineating
those various excellencies to which my heart and
feelings will however ever do justice. In a small
room appropriated to the purpose, and furnished
far more for comfort than for display, were we accustomed to assemble together to partake of our
morning meal after having been refreshed by the
sweet renovation of sleep. But the gratification of
our appetites was not the principal thing to which
my excellent father allowed our thoughts to be
directed. " Our *first* thoughts," said he, " must
be devoted to God. Afterwards we may . thank-
fully enjoy, in moderation, the good things which
he has mercifully sent to sustain us ;" and, accordingly, we all joined in supplicating for his gracious
aid and protection, and in expressing our gratitude
for various and manifold mercies. My eldest sis=
ter, Caroline, then took her station at the board ;
my mother occupied her right,—my father was
stationed at her left side,—and my youngest sister,
Phœbe, was disposed on the one opposite, while I
occupied the bottom of the table. And now I
must endeavour to give some insight into the characters of the several members composing this dear
family circle, beginning with the first mentioned,
and at this *one* hour of the day, perhaps the most
important personage present, when it is considered

that she was the dispenser of the refreshing beverage, which constituted a part of this delightful meal.   Caroline was by no means handsome : I believe she was by many thought decidedly plain ; but she was possessed of a countenance which, in my mind, constitutes the perfection of beauty, and needs no symmetry of feature to add to its interest. It expressed at once the intelligence of an acute mind, and the sensibility of a warm and tender heart.   It encouraged by its mildness, and delighted by its engaging sweetness, at the same time that it repressed any thing like unwarranted familiarity, by a certain gravity of expression, of which her whole demeanour also in some degree partook. Her manners were, however, kind and conciliatory, and though she never displayed very high or buoyant spirits, she was yet always cheerful, sometimes playful, and possessed of a calm and easy serenity of mind, which influenced all her actions. Her judgment was so clear, that when any point was debated in the family, it was generally in the end submitted to her decision ; and her upright principles, and distinct sense of right and wrong, fully justified this submission to her opinions.   She did not, however, appear aware of this almost insensible deference which was paid to them, or, if she was so, she was far too humble and too pious to allow it to give birth to arrogance or self-conceit.

I must next, I believe, touch upon my little
Phœbe, (as I was accustomed to call her,) as a
contrast in many points to her sister. She was all
life and vivacity, and the feelings of happy enthusiasm which she herself experíenced, she endeavoured to infuse into the hearts of all around her.
So open was her temper, and so cheerful her ideas,
that she could hardly conceive how any one could
be miserable or discontented, and so unsuspicious
was her nature that every thing was, in her opinion,
as fair as it appeared to be. Those whom she
either loved or admired were raised by her to the
pinnacle of absolute perfection, and it was therefore fortunate for her that as yet she had placed
her affections upon those only who would not abuse
them. This disposition gave her an almost continual flow of pleasurable emotions, but it incapa-
citated her from judging accurately of things or
persons, and rendered the advice and foresight of
others absolutely necessary. Her imagination was
quick and lively, and she possessed a considerable
degree of natural talent, which Caroline delighted
in encouraging and cultivating. She was, at this
time, about sixteen, and though not actually beautiful, she was yet so gay, so animated, and her
sparkling eyes and varying complexion bespoke so
truly the enthusiasm of her mind, that she was not
unfrequently called so. I need perhaps say little

C

of the form of such characters, when the characters themselves are known.   They will be perceived
to be at least amiable and good ; but they were also
vigilant and wise in training with prudent circumspection the young plants committed to their care,
endeavouring both to divest them of all disfiguring
excrescences, and to repress a too wanton luxuriance.   They both joined hand in hand, in maturing our expanding faculties, and storing our
youthful minds with lessons of virtue and morality,
and although their ideas and opinions were upon
many subjects essentially different, yet was this
never a source of jealousy or discord, for each was
anxious to please and oblige the other; and although
my mother's principal fault was an exceeding
warmth of temper, which even her excellent sense
had failed entirely to subdue, it yet always yielded
to the mild and affectionate remonstrances of my
father, and was accompanied too by such overflowing tenderness as made one almost forget that
it even existed.   My father had seen a great deal
of what is called the world, and his knowledge was
therefore derived from observation and experience,
as well as from study.   His conversational powers
were great, and, as he delighted in rendering every
instruction to his children, from him we derived a
great part of the general information which we
possessed.   We were in truth a most happy family;

and I love to look back to the days of my childhood, when blessed with such examples, and guided
by such councils. I, as being an only brother, was
perhaps rather too much indulged for my own good;
but, although it might create in me too great an
idea of my own importance, I trust it never rendered me ungrateful for the kindness I received,
or made me return it with unthankful moroseness.
In truth, I must have been insensible indeed, if
such had been my conduct. Such, however, being
the value, however unmerited, which was set upon
me, the reader may conceive the grief which was
felt by my family when death seemed ready to tear
me for ever from them; and what their anxiety,
when health was gradually returning, to accelerate
its progress by every means in their power. At
length, a scheme for that effect being digested, I
set out, followed by the prayers and good wishes
of my mother and sisters; and, accompanied by
my father, and our honest servant who had lived in
our family many years, and was become sincerely
attached to it, spent some weeks in travelling
about from one place to another, as my fancy or
my inclination led me. At the end of that time,
my father received a summons home, but, as he
imagined that I might receive benefit from an extension of our little tour, and as he placed great
confidence in the care and affection of our faithful

John, he desired that I would continue my wan-
derings a little longer, promising, if possible, towards the end of the autumn, to bring the rest of
my family to escort me back again. This arrangement made, he left me to my own free will, and
for some time I followed its dictates in going from
place to place in search of the beautiful, the romantic, and the picturesque in nature. I am naturally, (like my sister Phœbe,) rather enthusiastic,
and extremely susceptible of those impressions
which are made upon the mind by outward objects,
and which to me are sources of constant and ever-
varying pleasures. Alone in the wide field of
nature, with only the birds for my companions,
and all the garniture of this fair world for my study
and amusement, I feel a sweeter complacency and
joy reigning in my breast, than if I were in the
midst of society, and surrounded by gaiety and
pleasure.

One evening, when I had been at the small town
of —— for some days, employing my time in rambling through the adjacent country, and discovering
for myself numerous scenes of rural interest and
beauty ; having been out during the whole of the
morning, I resolved, after all the deliberation
which so important a question demanded, to spend
my evening in the little parlour which was appropriated to my use, at the *White Hart*, and amuse

myself with some one of my favourite authors.
Agreeably to this sage determination, I seated myself in the elbow chair which was placed on one side
of a bow window, commanding a view of a neat
little garden well stocked with all kinds of culinary
herbs, and ornamented with a flower border, whose
gay inhabitants diffused no inconsiderable fragrance
around. After sitting wrapt up in my own thoughts
for a few minutes, I exchanged them for those of
my author, and soon became wholly absorbed in
the deep interest which he excited. Soon, however, was the pleasing illusion most rudely dispelled by an unusual bustle and clamour which
proceeded from the room adjoining, where riotous
mirth and jollity seemed to prevail. In vain I endeavoured, by again resuming my book, to banish
these unwelcome sounds. They were far too distinct for me to lose them even for a moment.
At length, I rang my bell, and inquired, (I believe in no very amiable tone,) what caused this
unusual disturbance. " It is a party of young
men who are just arrived, Sir, and who are going
to their dinner." " How long do they mean to
remain ?" " I don't know indeed, Sir." " Very
well," replied I pettishly, and John disappeared.
Finding it utterly impossible to read in my room,
I put my book in my pocket, and going out at a
door which I perceived open at the back of the

house, proceeded through a narrow path which led
across some pretty looking fields, resolving to find
some secure spot where I could pursue my reading
without molestation. Having, however, fallen into
one of my usual reveries, I had proceeded almost
unconsciously for some distance, when I found myself before a little white cottage, which was situated
at the foot of a low hill that rose gradually behind
it, and embosomed in trees whose varied foliage,
now mellowed by the rich tints of autumn, presented a very lovely appearance. The cottage
itself was small, and wore rather a humble appearance, but the care with which the woodbines and
creepers were trained round the door seemed to bespeak some taste in its inmates, and the beautiful
neatness and cleanliness of the whole declared their
industry if not their superiority. As I was standing before this little mansion, admiring its appearance, I observed two females coming up a narrow
path which led from the back of the cottage, and
approaching towards the door. They seemed to
be walking very slowly, and, as they advanced, I
perceived that one was in bad health, and appeared
to be leaning for support on the other to whom my
whole attention was immediately directed. She
was in the bloom of youth, and in the meridian of
loveliness, and in her air and figure there was
something at once easy, dignified, and graceful.

Her head was at first turned towards her companion, whom she seemed to conduct with the most careful tenderness, and I saw only her snowy neck, and light waving tresses; but the moment that it was directed towards me, I beheld a countenance more sweet and prepossessing than any on which my sight had ever rested. It was not her features —I scarcely knew what they were—which instantaneously charmed me. It was the expression of feminine softness and delicacy, united with the flashing beams of intelligence, emitted by her expressive eyes, that touched my heart, as well as pleased my imagination. But I was not long allowed to gaze upon this beauteous vision, for almost immediately that she perceived me, she hastened in and closed the cottage door after her. In vain I waited near, in hopes of catching another, if but a momentary glance. I was not doomed to have my wishes gratified, and, at length, I retraced my steps to my little inn, torturing my fancy the whole way to discover who the lovely creature could be, residing in so obscure a dwelling, and vowing, in my own mind, that I would, in some way or other, gratify the inordinate curiosity which devoured me. Tired with my own fruitless suppositions, I again entered my room, and, finding that the riotous party which had before annoyed me were still carousing over the bottle,

I ascended to my bed-room, and retired to rest, to dream of the pretty cottage, and its interesting inhabitants.

The next morning, the first images which en-grossed my waking, were those which had occupied my sleeping fancy. A bright autumnal sun shot its piercing rays through my window, and invited by its beams, I sprang from my bed, and hastily dressing myself, descended to enjoy the invigorating influence of the morning air. But instead of taking my usual early walk, I was irresistibly impelled to visit the shop of a bookseller who lived near, and to whose circulating library I had sometimes since my arrival resorted for temporary amusement. In my visits for this purpose, I had been particularly pleased with the open-heartedness apparent in this man, and though his communicative propensities were rather too freely indulged, his evident good-nature, and wish of obliging, had always prevented my discovering the fatigue which I could not but feel at the repetition of sometimes even an already " twice told tale." Now, therefore, I rejoiced at my forbearance, and hoped to reap a reward by ob-taining from him some intelligence of the residents at the white cottage. I found my friend in his usual place behind the counter, but not wishing either to appear to have, or to excite too much curiosity, I first began to chat with him on other

subjects, until the one uppermost in my thoughts
was gradually introduced, and I discovered to my
great joy that I had applied to the very source for
obtaining the desired information. He told me
that the old lady and her daughter who lived at my
pretty cottage had not been long its inhabitants;
that their names were *Trevor*, but who they were,
or from whence they came, both himself and his
neighbours were entirely ignorant. " But as for
the young Miss, Sir, she is one of the prettiest and
best behaved ladies that I ever saw. She sometimes comes to my shop for a few books, to obtain
which, however, and even, as I suppose, the neces-
saries of life, she labours exceedingly hard. She
draws in a very superior style, and although this
small place, you know Sir, cannot be a good market
for such things, I nevertheless contrive to part with
a few of her most trifling pieces, and the remainder
I send to an agent in town, who easily disposes of
them." Some farther conversation ensued, but I obtained little more information concerning my " fair
unknown," and delighted with the proof which I believed I had got of her superiority and excellence, I
returned towards my inn, with my feelings of curio-.
sity and enthusiasm rather elevated than repressed.
" I was sure," said I to myself, " that that beaming
countenance indicated no ordinary mind, no vulgar
education ;" and, supremely happy in this evidence

of my own powers of penetration, I sat down to
my solitary breakfast with my appetite not a little
heightened by the new stimulus I had received,
and which seemed to have given a fresh spring both
to my mind and body.   There was a something so
novel, and at the same time so interesting, in the
whole affair, as was exactly fitted to seize on such
a susceptible imagination as mine; and that hair-
brained goddess, Fancy, carried me such endless
flights upon her airy wings, that my hostess, little
understanding, I conceive, the new regions into
which I had been travelling, began to think me an
inordinate time over my meal, and despatched my
valet to inquire " If his honour would like some
excellent pigeon-pie of her own making," as a hint,
I rather imagine, that I had already spent a sufficient time in the gratification of my palate.   The
reader will suppose that the pigeon-pie did not
make its appearance, but it had at least the merit
of awakening me from my trance, and I started up,
almost wondering at the hold which the white
cottage, the old lady, and the youthful stranger,
had taken on my mind.   Having first condescended
to answer my landlady's question of, " when would
I please to dine ?" and been even sufficiently common-place to settle of what my dinner should con-
sist, I took my usual companions, a book and my
walking-stick, and I believe instinctively followed

the path which I had discovered the preceding evening. For some paces, I walked at nearly the rate of ten miles an hour, as if the happiness of my future life depended on my arriving at the place of my destination by a certain moment. The image of my sister Phœbe first arrested my fleeting steps, by rushing to my mind's eye in the very act of laughing at her brother's folly,—" How the little merry gipsey would amuse herself at my expense," thought I, " and how would my sage father ridicule my adventure ¡" and my immoderate pace instantly reduced itself to a dilatory walk. " And after all," suggested that tormentor, Reason, " your beautiful unknown may descend from the pinnacle of perfection which you have raised for her, and be found to stand on the level plain, among a crowd of peasants and mechanics, and she may herself scrub her habitation, and nail up her creepers from a mere common-place love of neatness and cleanliness." " But no," retorted I aloud, with a triumphant air, and I believe I gave a very theatrical toss to my stick as I uttered the words—" No, that cannot be, for do I not know that she paints divinely! and had ever peasant-girl the air, the look, the manner, that she has?"—And my feelings of mortified despondency immediately gave way, as I remembered the information of my worthy friend, the bookseller. My step was again quickened as

before, and I had arrived within a field of the object
of my desire, when a loud scream burst upon my
ear, and I looked round, endeavouring to discover
from whence it could proceed. It was again repeated, and without further hesitation I ran as fast
as I could in the direction in which I thought it
came, and springing over a low hedge which appeared in my way, I beheld before my amazed
sight the lovely stranger kneeling before a young
and handsome man, who seemed to be trying forcibly to raise her from her abject position. I thought
I never witnessed so interesting a sight : her di-
shevelled hair was flowing down her neck in beautiful ringlets, her hands were raised in the act of
supplication, and in her countenance was depicted
the intense anguish which possessed her soul. The
moment, however, that she discovered me, she
sprang upon her feet, ran towards me, and in the
most piteous manner implored my assistance. But
before I could reply to her moving entreaties, she,
as if suddenly recollecting herself, and the momentary elation of hope which had illuminated her face at
my appearance flying away like a passing sun-beam,
changed her look of supplication into one of commanding dignity, as turning towards the stranger,
whom I had as yet scarcely noticed,—" Unless, Sir
Edward," said she, " this is one of the *worthy* companions of whom you boast, and whom you have

prepared to assist you in your *honourable* and
humane purpose of destroying for ever the happiness of a poor, unprotected, fatherless young creature—" Here some inward emotion seemed to
struggle with her efforts to preserve herself calm
and self-possessed, till again approaching me, she
added, in the most solemn accents, and which
seemed to thrill through my very heart as she uttered them,—" I adjure you by all that is good
and sacred, not to load your soul with the heavy guilt
of having assisted in the destruction of a helpless
female ; and in the name of innocence and virtue,
I beseech you to protect me against the violence of
this bad man !" So wonderfully impressive was
the manner of this young creature, that until this
moment I had not the power of uttering a single
syllable, and it appeared that it had the same effect
on her persecutor, who had remained on the spot in
which I found him, either as if spell-bound by her
words, or as unknowing in what way to act. Now,
however, before I could explain to her, her mistake
as to my character, he rushed impetuously forward,
and seizing her by the arm, swore " that she was
his, that nothing should part them, and that he
dared me to attempt her rescue." " Oh no, no,"
exclaimed she, " believe him not, he is nothing to
me but at once my dread and my abhorrence !" I
immediately calmed her apprehensions by vowing

to protect her from injury, and I then demanded of
the gentleman an explanation of the right by which
he detained her, so obviously against her wish and
inclination.   To this he was prevented replying
by her suddenly, and, as if with supernatural
strength, disengaging herself from his grasp, and
flying up a narrow path which I supposed led to
the cottage, as I observed a part of it just peeping
above the trees.   He attempted to follow and overtake her, but I immediately placed myself in his
way, and told him on his peril to stir farther in his
evidently nefarious purpose.   At first he made use
of high words and opprobrious language, but I
could easily perceive that he was as cowardly as
brutal, and that he was only attempting to bully
me out of the part that I was taking.   I therefore
took out my card, and informed him of my present
abode, adding that I should be ready at any time
when he chose to require it, to give an explanation
of my present conduct, but that I again insisted on
his giving up all idea of following the young lady
whom I had the honour of assisting.   At this fortunate moment, I perceived the broad and sturdy
figure of my valiant Squire passing along the adjoining field, and calling loudly to him until I perceived that he heard and was approaching me, I
farther added, " And now, Sir, if you do not
choose quietly to leave this spot, I must engage my

servant to assist me in protecting the lady from
farther insult; if on the contrary, you take the
wiser part, I repeat that I shall be ready at any
moment to answer your inquiries at my inn, whither
I shall probably return in a few hours." All this
time, my opponent seemed uncertain whether or not
to give up the contest, his inclination evidently
prompting him to do the former, but false shame
appearing to hold him back irresolute. When,
however, John, (who had followed me with a despatch from my father,) having nearly arrived at the
spot where we stood, the suggestions of fear overcame all others, and muttering something of " re-
venge," — and " ungentlemanly conduct," — this
Achilles turned on his heel, and walked sullenly
away. Having received my letter and deposited it
safely in my pocket, I followed as quickly as possible the path which my " fair one " had pursued,
and which I found did indeed terminate at the
the cottage. It immediately occurred to me, however, that it would be indelicate in me to force
myself into her presence, more especially when she
might perhaps feel some sense of obligation, and
yet I was anxious to learn whether she were really
arrived safely at home, as it appeared that her persecutor was accompanied by companions, who might
for all I knew, be likewise way-laying her. A
dread of not again meeting with her, and curiosity

to learn what circumstances could have led to the
scene which I had just witnessed, also conspired to
prompt me to seize the present opportunity.   At
last, however, I wisely resolved to take a middle
course, and to send my servant with a hastily
written note, containing the following lines:—

" Mr. ——————— begs to know if he can be of
any farther service to Miss Trevor, as he shall be
most happy to execute any commands which she
may have for him.   He hopes that she is quite
recovered from the effects of her late alarm, with a
repetition of which he thinks he may venture to
promise her she shall not be troubled."

If the reader ever felt the anxiety attendant upon
an enthusiastic mind just seized upon by some new
interest which it knows not will be answered or acknowledged, and is even at a loss how to express
—ignorant, in fine, whether he may not be absorbed by an object of no importance but in his
own inflammable fancy,—he will know how to understand the nervous and impatient feelings with
which I was tortured, while John was executing
my commission.   At one moment I blamed myself
for my final decision, and thought of my sister
Phœbe's favourite maxim, that " boldness alone
would eventually ensure the success of any design;"
repenting that I had not appeared in *propriâ per-
sona*, and satisfied myself whether or not my ima-

gination was indeed torturing or obscuring simple realities. In the next, perhaps, I applauded my own self-denial, and felt certain that it would be properly appreciated; and, at last, by an unaccountable impulsion of mind, I resigned myself into the depths of utter despair, and was endeavouring, with all the coolness of a philosopher, to acquire resignation to bear the frustration of my hopes, by convincing myself of the certainty of their being disappointed, when my servant again appeared, bearing "compliments" from Mrs. Trevor, and a message which intimated that she would be obliged by the favour of a call; and then, what became of the boasted indifference which I thought I had just attained, either to the success or denial of my wishes?——I certainly did not stay to solve the problem, for in three minutes more I found myself at the door of the *pretty cottage*.

With a palpitating heart, I announced my arrival, and my summons for admittance was answered by a neat little girl, apparently about fourteen or fifteen years of age, whom I afterwards discovered to be the only domestic. Her face crimsoned, as she cast a sheepish side-glance upon my figure, and, with a courtesy in which modesty and awkwardness were blended, ushered me, with a " Be pleased to walk this way, Sir," into a room which corresponded in its extreme neatness with the whole

D

appearance of the cottage. It was empty; but, at first, I was too much engaged with one idea, that of again beholding my interesting fair one, to take more than a general survey of its contents. As, however, it was some minutes before my solitude was broken in upon, I had time to collect my scattered thoughts, and to examine more minutely the several objects around me. This, in truth, was no work of labour. The furniture was all of the simplest description. There was enough for comfort, but nothing for the purposes of luxury or indulgence, save indeed one large chair, which seemed intended to give a feeling of greater ease than its fellows, and which confirmed the idea which I had formed of the feebleness of the elder lady. But, although every thing was thus plain and humble, there was a something in the disposal of all which showed an attention to appearance, and a wish of setting off the whole to the best advantage. On the chimney-piece were one or two ornaments, constructed, I made no doubt, by the fair hands of Miss Trevor, and a few flowers were tastefully disposed, and filled the air with their fragrance. In one corner also stood a small book-case, in which I perceived some of the best authors in the English, and a few in the French and Italian languages, and on a table lay materials for painting, which seemed to have been lately in use. I ventured to

take up a sketch which was half covered with a
piece of paper, and, as I did so, I saw on another
a few lines written in a neat and indeed elegant
hand. I had just replaced the former, after admiring the masterly style in which it was executed,
when the door opened, and a lady entered,—but it
was not Miss Trevor, and I returned her salutation
with a feeling of inexpressible disappointment.
This, however, was only the feeling of the moment, for in truth the appearance and manners of
the mother were almost as interesting as those of
the daughter. She was apparently in ill health,
and her countenance bore the traces of recent suffering ; but its melancholy expression was mingled
with so much of goodness as well as intelligence as
in an instant to charm the eye, and touch the heart
of the beholder. She evidently had been handsome, and even now she merited the appellation of
" a fine woman ;" and there was something in her
whole gait and deportment which appeared to say,
" I am not what I seem," unattended however by
any thing approaching to stiffness or *hauteur*.
When we were both seated, she commenced the
conversation by thanking me in warm and even
eloquent terms, for the assistance which I had rendered to her " dear child," while a glow spread
over her pale cheek, and tears started into her
expressive eyes as she declared she should ever

consider me as the deliverer of that child from
misery.   I endeavoured to disclaim all merit in the
affair, alleging, what was indeed true, that the
part which I had taken was merely that which
common humanity dictated, and one which every
one with the feelings of a gentleman was bound to
perform.   She smiled at what she was pleased to
term " my humility," but declared, that both herself
and her daughter should ever consider themselves
as under a heavy debt of gratitude to me for the
aid which I had so opportunely afforded.   " And
now," added she, " *that* gratitude to yourself, and
justice to my dear Louisa, demand that I should
explain the extraordinary situation in which you
discovered her, to account for which, I must touch
slightly upon some former events of my life,
which, however, I trust you will excuse."   I assured her how much I felt gratified by her con-
descending thus to inform me of what I had even
no pretence f. demanding, and, at the same time,
telling her, that I wanted no assurances to convince me, that no blame could possibly attach to
Miss Trevor in the disgraceful scene which I had
witnessed, as I had myself seen displayed a purity
and heroism of conduct which could have sprung
only fro a noble and a virtuous mind.   As I pro
nounced ese words, I saw her bending on me an
earnest and inquisitive gaze, as if she would fain

have searched my heart, and discovered my character, but this was almost immediately succeeded by one which I fancied I could interpret in my favour, as she thanked me for the indulgent light in which I viewed what might perhaps reasonably give birth to suspicion, and then began her narration as follows : " I have only lost my husband, Sir, a few years. Before his death, we were plentifully blessed with the goods of fortune. I had then two children : my dear Louisa, and her brother Charles, now alas ! no more. As the former was accustomed to mix much in society, and was expected to be possessed of a considerable fortune, she naturally excited some attention, and several offers were made for her hand. Among her suitors was Sir Edward Stanley, the young man whom you beheld this morning. He was the most assiduous in his attentions to her, and, from his rank and situation in life, which he knows how to value, added to a good person and insinuating manners, neither of which does he either by any means underrate, he considered himself, I believe, pretty certain of success. But he is dissipated, frivolous, and vain. Virtue does not restrain, principle does not actuate him ; and Louisa could not be caught by mere personal graces, or sacrifice herself to obtain an addition of rank. He was rejected, but not daunted, and he long continued

to torment her with his suit ; until, at length,
convinced by her steady and uniformly repelling
conduct, that she really intended to refuse him,
his mortified vanity prompted him to show his
sense of the supposed indignity which had been
offered him. It suffices to say, that in consequence,
in a great measure, of his secret machinations, my
husband was ruined, and died of a broken heart,
at beholding his family hurled from a state of affluence into one of poverty. My son was carried
off by a lingering decline, and my own health was
severely shattered by the train of misfortunes
which so rapidly succeeded each other. My beloved
Louisa alone," added she, " could have enabled
me to support the load of existence, but, for her
sake, may it please the Almighty yet for a little
while to preserve it to me. Well," continued she,
resuming the calmness which the strong tide of
maternal affection had for a moment disturbed,
" now to the point before us. This morning my
daughter was going to town, as she frequently does,
to transact any little business with which our servant cannot be trusted, when she was suddenly met
by Sir Edward Stanley, who appeared so little surprised at seeing her, that she supposed that he
must, by some means or other, have discovered our
abode, although, partly from the dread of his farther persecutions, we have endeavoured as much as

possible to conceal it. He approached her with the utmost freedom, and dared to address her in the same strain of love as formerly, with however still less restraint or delicacy. With the remembrance of her father's unmerited injuries uppermost in her mind, you cannot wonder that she recoiled from him with horror, and displayed in her answer the disgust and abhorrence with which he had inspired her. Enraged at her manner, and stung, I suppose, by her just reproaches, his language became still more free and even violent. In fine, the wretch had the audacity to make proposals which filled her soul with horror, and, assuring her that he had friends near who would assist him in executing his purpose, he endeavoured to force her to accompany him to a carriage, which, he said, was waiting in the adjacent road; and, frantic with the dread of her own fate, and her mother's anguish, on hearing that her only stay was thus dragged from under her, she sunk on her knees before this brute in human form, and implored him to have pity upon her helpless condition. Here, directed no doubt by a gracious Providence, you arrived to save her from infamy and me from a broken heart; and Heaven," added she emphatically, " Heaven, which led you thither, will also bless and reward you." She then said that her daughter had earnestly begged her to express the grateful feelings

with which she was impressed, and to make her
excuses for not declaring them in person, as she
was at present too unwell from the hurry and fright
which she had received. I confess that I experienced a twinge of disappointment on hearing this,
although it was what I had partly anticipated.
I was, however, too polite, or, perhaps, too politic,
to discover this feeling; and, charmed with the
kind of confidence which Mrs. Trevor had placed
in me, I in return gave her an account of myself
and my family, adding, that I hoped the latter
would soon join me, when I should have the pleasure of introducing to her all its members. While
I was speaking, I observed that her countenance
underwent constant variations, for which I was
unable to account. At first, some thought seemed
to rush upon her mind which awakened anxious
expectation. This was succeeded by close and
eager attention; and, lastly, followed by a calm
and settled expression of complacency as I concluded. Then, with mingled courtesy and delight, she held out her hand. " With sincere
pleasure," said she, " I claim you as a relation.
Had not my thoughts been so completely engaged
by one subject, I should probably have been led
by your name to suspect the truth. You have,
perhaps, heard me mentioned by your father, with
whom I was very intimate in former days. He

is my cousin, and gladly do I recognise in you the son of so excellent a man." " Good heavens !" I exclaimed, " and are you indeed that beloved cousin after whom he has made so many fruitless inquiries ? How could I possibly be so stupid as not to divine this before !" I then explained to her that my father had been abroad for some years, during which, the changes which she had mentioned had taken place in her family, and that, on his return, he had been unable to discover the place of her abode. " But why, my dear Madam," added I, " why have you so entirely secluded yourself from your friends ? Excuse my question, but I feel of how much pleasure you have deprived them." " Your question is natural," replied she, " for you have not suffered by the reverses of fortune. While in prosperity, I was courted and sought after, but when the chill winds of adversity blew around me, I was left to encounter their pitiless violence alone. I never before felt the selfishness and versatility of the world. The late-discovered truth stunned me. My son was torn from me by death, and sorrow which sought repose, and I fear false pride which courted concealment, led me hither. One friend only knows the place of my retreat, and although I have for Louisa's sake repented the indulgence which I have allowed to my feelings, I have never yet had courage to proclaim myself to those whom I yet know would truly participate in my sorrows. The hand of Providence is visible. I was proud, and I am humbled. I murmured, but I have been taught resignation. I *have* suffered, but I *am* thankful." Her countenance beamed with the heavenly spirit which animated her, and, as I beheld the workings of that spirit, I could not but exclaim to myself, " sweet indeed *are* the uses of adversity." Much interesting conversation succeeded, in which I thought I could perceive a naturally strong and susceptible mind which had received a severe shock, but which now rested secure upon the " rock of ages ;" and whose brightness, obscured only for a season by the cloud which had gathered over it, now shone forth with increased and more durable splendour. On taking my leave, I requested permission to call on the ensuing day, saying, that I then hoped to be able to bring ample apologies from Sir Edward Stanley for his unmanly conduct. She cast on me a look of mingled alarm and approbation. " We are already greatly your debtors," said she, " and your kindness would increase the obligation, but you must allow me to insist that you proceed no farther in this business. We must trust to our own prudence and caution for our future safety, and remember that our anxiety would be greatly increased if we thought that

a relation so newly found, should be drawn into
any uncomfortable situation through our means."
I begged her not to fear this being at all the case ;
and, leaving a respectful message for Miss Trevor,
I summoned courage to leave a place which presented to me so many charms, and whose inhabitants seemed more and more to interest my feelings
as I became farther acquainted with them.

My unwilling feet, sympathizing I suppose with
my thwarted inclination, carried me very slowly
back to my own apartment, which appeared unusually lonely and desolate ; and in vain did I
resort to my books for amusement to while away
the hours which must intervene before dinner (that
excellent divider of the day to which the idle man
looks with such extreme complacency,) arrived.
My thoughts still wandered to the white cottage,
and my memory still conjured up the forms of the
sweet Louisa and her interesting parent.   At last,
I remembered the despatch which my servant had
so opportunely brought me a few hours before, and
denouncing myself as an ungrateful son, I tore
open my father's letter with eager impatience.
The contents were of a mixed nature.   They informed me that my father intended speedily joining
me at ———, but added, that the illness of one of
my sisters prevented my mother from accompanying him ; and, although I was grieved at her being

deprived of an excursion which appeared likely to
have afforded her pleasure, I could not but feel
great delight at the prospect of my father's almost
immediate arrival.

My thoughts now recurred to the events of
the morning, and I began to consider what steps
I should pursue to obtain the acknowledgment
which I desired from Sir Edward Stanley. As
he considered his honour wounded by my interference, he would probably, I thought, demand
satisfaction at my hands; but as I held the system
of duelling in utter abhorrence, I resolved to avoid
such an issue to the affair by every means consistent
with my own character and the safety of Miss
Trevor, and I conceived from what I had already
observed of my adversary, that he would not be
disposed to risk his person without an absolute ne-
cessity. While I was thus deliberating, a gentleman was announced, who proved, as I expected, to
be commissioned to desire an explanation of my
" ungentlemanly interference, in a matter which
could in no wise concern me." "Tell your friend,"
answered I, " that I consider every man who is
endued with the feelings of justice and humanity as
concerned in protecting injured innocence, and in
rescuing helpless virtue from the hands of brutality
and cruelty. Tell him that such is the only explanation which I shall give, or he can require, of my

conduct, and as I was most fortunately enabled to frustrate his designs, so I demand from him, in the name óf Miss Trevor, an ample apology for his behaviour, and a pledge that it shall not be repeated." The young gentleman seemed as if almost ashamed of the part which he was taking in the business, although he thought it necessary to say, that he came to receive, not to be asked for an apology. " I cannot, Sir," answered I, " apologize for a conduct which my own heart tells me was right, and as Sir Edward Stanley must be aware that his own was most unjustifiable, I hope that he will have the candour and good sense to acknowledge it." " Why, 'pon my faith, Sir, it seems a confounded thing to measure swords upon such a d——d nonsensical affair as this," rejoined my sapient companion, " so I'll e'en tell my friend what you say, before I deliver the message with which I was charged:" and so saying, with an air of the most perfect self-complaisance, my coxcomical visitor disappeared. I soon heard Sir Edward blustering at what he termed my insolence, and swearing that he would be revenged. He was answered by one or two of his companions, who I imagined were endeavouring to dissuade him from proceeding to violence. He then seemed to be angry with his friend for not having delivered his challenge, when the latter answered him at some

length, and I heard him reply, " Ah, true Jack,
the fellow won't be here long; its hardly worth
while to run the risk of having one's throat cut,
and losing the girl too, and so,"——Here the door
of the adjoining apartment was closed, and I heard
no more; but as I suspected that he still purposed
to follow up his diabolical design, I resolved to
demand a decided promise of its relinquishment.
In about five minutes, the former messenger appeared, bearing an apology from his friend to the
lady for his behaviour, which he protested was
caused by the violence of his passion, and assuring
her of his grief at having been so unhappy as to
give her a moment's uneasiness. " But, Sir," said
I, looking fixedly in his countenance, " this does
not secure her from a repetition of Sir Edward's
attempts, and I must insist upon an assurance that
she shall for the future be entirely free from them."
" What possible right can you have to dictate to
Sir Edward Stanley in this way, Sir," retorted my
companion, endeavouring to put on a fierce aspect,
for which however his insignificant visage was ill
calculated. " The same right, Sir," replied I,
" which I before observed that every man has of defending the innocent and the helpless. I have also
the honour of being related to Miss Trevor, and as
her relation, I demand a promise that she shall be
no farther molested." " Very extraordinary, 'pon

honour, Sir, that a gentleman is thus to have his proceedings shackled! — However," added he, drawing himself up, and surveying himself in a glass which was hung up opposite to him, "as Miss Trevor is not the only young lady who blesses mankind with her presence, I believe my friend will not trouble himself to contend farther for the beauteous prize." "I am to understand, then, Sir, that Miss Trevor may be entirely free from all apprehensions on this account?" "You are, Sir." "That then is sufficient, as I conceive myself to be dealing with men of honour." The young fop had the grace to look half confused as I emphatically pronounced these words, and twirling round a riding-stick, which had been of no small assistance to him in this interview, he made his exit, to all appearance glad of having terminated his errand.

A few minutes after he had taken his departure, my servant entered with a note which he informed me was brought by a girl, who waited for an answer. Judging that it came from my new friends, I eagerly snatched the billet, and first glancing at the signature, saw as I hoped, the name of Trevor. It was from Mrs. Trevor herself, and expressed the uneasiness which she said she had experienced ever since my departure in the morning, as she could not help fearing that some unpleasant consequences would ensue from the affair in which I had so humanely engaged. She therefore begged me to ease her mind with an assurance that I would let the matter rest where it now stood, without taking any farther steps which my kindness or my resentment might prompt. Glad of an excuse for paying a second visit to the cottage, I resolved to deliver my answer in person, and I soon found myself at full speed on the way to my place of destination. When I came within sight of the humble little dwelling, my heart began to palpitate most strangely, and, eagerly as I had proceeded but a few moments before, I now paused and hesitated as if I was on the eve of performing the most disagreeable task in the world. At length, mustering my abundant stock of courageous boldness, I opened the little wicket-gate which led into the garden, and advanced towards the door. Mrs. Trevor, who I suppose had perceived my approach, appeared there to welcome me, and all my foolish tremors were put to rest by the warmth and open cordiality of her manners. " I have just sent a few lines to you," said she, " to beg,—but probably you have arrested my messenger, and are acquainted with their purport." I told her that my present visit was caused by the kind anxiety which she had expressed on my account, and I was proceeding to explain to her what had passed with Sir Edward Stanley, when she ushered me into her

little sitting-room, where the first object I beheld
was the fair Louisa, who rose with alacrity on my
entrance, though her face became, for an instant,
suffused with blushes, while she returned my greet-
ing. In a moment afterwards, however, the confusion which was visible disappeared, and with an
air of graceful ease and dignity which seemed to
be natural to her, she thanked me with that unaffected warmth which a susceptible and ingenuous
mind alone can dictate, neither attempting to disguise her own grateful feelings, nor paining or op-
pressing me by an useless expression of them. I
then changed the current of conversation, by deli-
vering the message with which I was charged, and
which seemed to give both the ladies great satisfaction, and by informing them of the contents of
my father's letter. A general but interesting conversation ensued, in which although Miss Trevor
took no very active part, yet all that she did say, was
distinguished by so much good sense and propriety
of feeling, that I was beyond measure delighted.
Literary subjects were gradually introduced, and
although far from attempting any thing like display, she joined as little as possible in our dis-
cussion, it was yet evident from the observations
which she occasionally made, and the remarks
which she hazarded, that she possessed considerable depth of thought and observation, and that her

E

mental powers had been highly cultivated. Having remained as long as my conscience would allow me, I again took my leave, more than ever pleased with my new friends, and so agreeably had the time passed in their society, that I was perfectly amazed to find how far the evening had waned, and how rapidly the dark shades of night were advancing.

The next morning I summoned to my aid all the stock of philosophy of which I was master, resolving that day not to visit the cottage, which I thought would be taking undue advantage of the feelings which were at present existing in my favour in the breasts of its inhabitants. " My father," considered I, " will soon be here, and will no doubt renew his former intimacy and friendship with Mrs. Trevor; till then, therefore, I will be contented to absent myself." Pursuant to this sage and praiseworthy determination, I constrained myself to pursue my rambles in an exactly opposite direction to that to which my wishes pointed, although every step I took seemed to cause me unusual labour and fatigue, and the same scenery which had appeared to me a few days before so glowing and beautiful, was now tame and insipid; for then my mind was alive only to the loveliness of nature, and now it was engaged by other objects to which it pertinaciously adhered. I endeavoured to explain to myself why it was that they thus engaged my thoughts, and fastened upon my imagination, but I could at last only solve the difficulty by supposing that my naturally enthusiastic fancy had been pleased with the novelty of the late adventure, and that my ideas having been so long wandering in all directions, had eagerly settled upon the first resting-place which offered itself.

Finding it utterly impossible for me to remain quietly in the house, I again sallied forth in the evening ; but I had still sufficient resolution to avoid taking the course which my inclination directed, and I turned in a nearly parallel, but still different direction, towards a romantic little village which had frequently attracted me before. After walking about a mile and a half through some of the prettiest fields imaginable, I saw the tops of the cottages peeping through the trees; and in a few minutes more, I found myself in the principal street, (if street it might be called) where the neat little dwellings which composed it were each surrounded by a little garden in which the old trees were bending under their load of fruit, which was fast ripening through the powerful influence of an autumnal sun. It was just at that time in the evening when the cottagers, having performed all the labours of the day, were sitting at their doors, enjoying the mildness of the atmosphere, and partaking of perhaps their only relaxation, a gossip

with their friends and neighbours.   Most of them
presented a clean and pleasing appearance, without
any of the dirt and wretchedness which are but too
observable among the lower class of inhabitants of
a large town, or even of a village adjacent to any
populous city.   I passed on, inwardly participating
in the peaceful serenity of the scene, and amused at
the observation and speculations which I seemed to
excite, until I arrived at the far end of the village,
looking into the humble dwellings as I passed, and
entertaining myself by contrasting the various appearances which they exhibited.   Finding that it
was not late, I thought I would proceed still a little
farther; and observing a walk across some fields
which seemed to lead towards the village church,
which I beheld at a little distance, I followed the
path and soon arrived at this simple house of God,
which presented more charms to my mind than the
handsome and sculptured edifices which I had seen
also devoted to the service of the same great Being;
for there was something here which conveyed to
me ideas of pious simplicity which they could not
awaken.   " Here," thought I to myself, " man
appears the insignificant thing he really is.—
There, his weak mind is too apt to be elated
by the (to him) vast monuments of his genius
which he sees around him.—There, I *may* think
of God.—Here, I think *only* of him.

Some sweet little children were playing before the doors of a cottage or two which stood near me; and, as even the sports of childhood are frequently to me subjects of interest, I stood for some time watching the motions of the little urchins, and contrasting their fine healthy colour and open countenances with the wan emaciated faces of those who are obliged to be confined in close and narrow streets. Notwithstanding the deceptious nature of feeling and appearance, however, I soon found that even here lurked in embryo some of the bad passions of human nature. One very pretty boy was whipping a top, when one much older than himself came and snatched it from him, and continued to tease the poor little fellow, who, in vain, begged him to return it. Some of his companions at last espoused his cause, and commanded his adversary to restore to him the stolen treasure, till, enraged at the menaces which they employed, he threw the top with violence upon the stones, and broke it. The poor little boy, seeing his beloved plaything not only wrested from him but destroyed, could not contain his grief, and he sobbed with as much anguish as if he had lost a kingdom, for it was by him as highly and perhaps more justly valued. After reproving the elder boy for the wanton and ill-natured action of which he had been guilty, I soon dried up the tears of his injured companion, by giving him money to purchase another top; and, unable to express his delight and gratitude, he ran into the cottage near him to tell his mother how good the gentleman had been to him. He was proceeding to tell his tale, when I heard a gentle voice exclaim, " Hush! my dear boy, your mother is too ill to hear you." I hastened in—I could not be mistaken,—it was Louisa,—not as I first beheld her, supporting her parent with tender care, or as I again saw her, paralyzed with terror at the feet of the villain Stanley; but bending, like a ministering angel, over the bed of sickness, and soothing the apparently dying moments of a fellow-creature. " Beautiful, I thought thee before," said I to myself, " but never couldst thou appear one-half so lovely in my eyes, as while thus obeying the sweet dictates of humanity, and the precepts of the Christian religion." She was kneeling before a lowly pallet, on which was extended the almost lifeless body of her charge, whose head she supported with one hand, while the other held a book, in which she appeared to have been reading. I could contemplate her but for a moment;—she turned round at my step, and again were her cheeks tinged with blushes;—but they were now those of detected virtue, which sought the silent shade where it might bloom unseen,—before, they were the bright tints of genuine modesty. Self

was, however, with her but a secondary object;
and, although confused at this discovery of her
own charitable kindness, she did not for a moment forget the wants of the poor sufferer before her, who now opened her eyes, and looked
up in her face with an expression of deep gratitude, which will never be effaced from my
memory. Louisa turned to me with a languid
smile, and beckoned me towards her. In an instant I was by her side. " I fear," said she, in
a low voice, " I fear this poor woman is very
near her end. Will you oblige me by going to
Mr. White, the clergyman, and begging him to
come to her immediately?" I ventured to press
her hand in reply, for my heart was too full for
speech; and then, repenting of my own temerity,
I hurried out of the cottage. The little boy followed me, crying as if his heart would break,
though he scarcely knew for what, but that his
mother had been accustomed to listen to a detail of
all his little joys and sorrows, and now she could
do neither. I soon contrived to cheer him; and
making him show me the road to the parsonage,
I proceeded thither with all possible haste. A gen-
tlemanly looking old man, whose countenance was
illuminated by the sunshine of benevolence, was
amusing himself in a neatly-disposed garden before
a simple but comfortable dwelling. " That is our

parson, Sir," said my little companion, and I immediately went up to him, and told my errand, while he, on the other hand, immediately desisted from his employment, snatched up his hat, and followed me without uttering a syllable, until he was really on his road towards the cottage. He then expressed his surprise at hearing that his poor parishioner was in so deplorable a state, as he had seen her early in the morning, and found her much better than usual. I asked her complaint, which he informed me was consumption,—that she was a clean, industrious, and respectable woman, but had unfortunately married a man destitute of every principle, who had at last deserted her, since which time she had contrived to support herself and child by her labour, though grief and hard living had so great an effect upon a naturally delicate constitution as to carry her to an untimely grave. " For," added he, " even if she is not in the immediate danger which you represent, it is impossible, without a manifest interposition of Providence in her behalf, that she can struggle much longer with her malady. From the deceitful appearances of the complaint under which she is suffering, one would indeed be sometimes almost tempted to think that she might eventually recover, but these are only the bright but transient rays emitted at intervals by the expiring lamp of life ere it is finally extinguished." " But, let us hope," said the worthy pastor, lifting up his eyes to heaven with a look of radiant but humble hope, " only to be rekindled for ever in the regions of immortality. Providence," continued he, turning to me again, " sent to this poor woman in her utmost need, a guide and comforter, under the form of a young and tender female who has been no less the directress of her mind, than the attendant upon her weak and enfeebled frame. Under her tuition, she has learnt to draw unceasing draughts of consolation from that fountain at which alone they must be sought, and to raise her thoughts from the toils and troubles of this world, to rest them in humble confidence upon the mercy-seat of the Most High. This has been the blessed work, as I before said, of a very young lady, whose soul seems to be the seat of almost every Christian virtue, and who has evidently studied, and profited well by the book of life and revelation. But I need hardly say all this to you, Sir, as, from your acquaintance with this poor woman, you probably know her fair instructress." He smiled, as he uttered these words, either at something suggested by his own imagination, or at observing the fixed, indeed delighted attention, with which I listened to his eulogium upon the lovely Louisa. From some feeling which was incomprehensible to myself, I had not yet men-

tioned her name, although I had resolved to do so
from the first moment that I beheld the venerable
Mr. White. I now, however, told him, that I
had but a very short time had the happiness of
being known to her, informing him likewise of the
relationship which subsisted between us. " Neither have I," replied he, " been long acquainted
with Miss Trevor. I first met her a few months
ago at the cottage to which we are going, and,
charmed by her active and well-directed benevolence, I assisted her as much as I could in her
work of charity ; and the better I knew, the more
was I astonished at the prudence and wisdom which
she displayed far beyond her years, and which,
superadded to her zeal in the cause of religion,
have led to the most happy results. And though,
I at once discovered that she, like myself, possessed not the goods of fortune in sufficient abundance to render much pecuniary assistance to the
object of her benevolence, yet, because she is
denied their aid, she does not neglect all the other
means of doing good which are in the power of
every human being ; and, if not able to cure the
distresses of poverty, she softens and alleviates
them, by teaching how best they may be borne."
" But here we are," continued the old man, as we
arrived at the cottage, " and here too," turning on
me an arch look, which made me look ineffably

silly, " is my fair coadjutress," extending his hand
to Miss Trevor, who shook it cordially. Her poor
charge had fallen into a gentle slumber, and anxious not to disturb her, we preserved the most
profound quiet. " I fear, my dear Sir," said
Louisa, " that our patient cannot last through the
night, and, as she has no one near her but the
surrounding neighbours, I cannot think of leaving
her. I took the liberty of sending for you, because I felt that you could more effectually admi-
nister to her that spiritual comfort, at which I can
but poorly endeavour. But since she is at present
unable to attend to you, perhaps you will kindly
write a line to my mother to explain the cause of my
prolonged absence." " Assuredly, my dear young
lady, I will do so," said he, and he took a pencil
out of his pocket for the purpose, when I interposed, begging that I might be allowed to be the
bearer of a message to Mrs. Trevor, which I said
might perhaps be still farther satisfactory to her ;
" unless," added I, turning to Mr. White, " I can
be employed in any way more useful." " You are
very good to devote your time to my service, young
gentleman," said the reverend man, with a sly
smile playing for a moment on his lip, " but," he
continued seriously, " I believe we can do all for
this poor soul which she may require. I will
remain with my young friend here, who, I am

sure will be infinitely obliged to you, if you will
undertake to put her mother's mind at ease on her
account." She smiled as she expressed her thoughts,
and I thought I saw another blush cross her interesting features.   At any rate, both the smile and the
blush served as food for my meditative powers for
some distance, until they were forgotten in dwelling
upon the proofs which I had this evening received
of the excellence of her heart and her principles.

I found Mrs. Trevor very anxious at her daughter's protracted stay ; but when I explained its
cause, and informed her of the intention of
Mr. White to remain as her companion, her uneasiness was instantly dissipated, and she evidently
highly approved of Louisa's intention of remaining
at the cottage.   For her's was not a false and selfish affection which would keep the object of its
love from the performance of a duty, for the sake
of its own indulgence, but one which received its
highest gratification from beholding that object
pursuing the path of virtue, however difficult,
however dangerous.   At length, I unwillingly returned to my solitary abode, resolving to hasten
to the village of ——— by break of day, and inquire
the state of the poor sick woman.

Accordingly, with the first approaches of bright-
eyed Phœbus, I sprang from my restless couch,
and sallied forth again with eager step.   The

cottage door was closed, but when I gently rapped, it was opened by a decent-looking woman, who immediately informed me that her poor neighbour was dead, and that Miss Trevor had left about five minutes before, taking with her the little destitute boy who had so much interested me. " Blessings light on her," said the woman, " for never was there a better-hearted lady in the world, and she deserves to have the *fortin* of a princess, for she'd do nothing but good with it." My hand, which had involuntarily found its way into my pocket during this artless speech, returned with a crown-piece, and while the astonished dame dropped a low curtesy, and attempted to utter her thanks for what appeared to her, I suppose, such unexampled bounty; now, thought I exultingly, will my name be joined with *her's* by one human being at least, and mine and Louisa's will be united in the praises of this poor woman. Was this charity? or the selfish gratification of feeling? I fear to define it with precision.

In pursuance of a plan which I had already formed in my own mind, I resolved that my next object should be the parsonage; but, as the present was too unseasonable an hour for a visit there, I wandered about until I thought I might hope to see its reverend owner, whom I found with his wife and three fine healthy children, seated round

the breakfast table. I was heartily invited to
partake of their meal, and readily closed with a
proposal which exercise had rendered unusually
welcome. At the conclusion of our repast, which
was graced by ease, cheerfulness, and good humour, the old gentleman led me into his study,
and acquainted me with the particulars of the
death of his poor parishioner. I then stated, that
unless I interfered with his arrangements, I was
very anxious to do something for her poor friendless
boy, and begged his advice as to the measures
which it was best for his future welfare to pursue.
His eyes glistened at this proposal which he readily
and joyfully accepted. " I have, indeed," said
he, " been puzzled as to what measures I could
take in favour of this poor unfortunate child. I
have not the means of providing for him entirely
myself, neither has his present kind protectress,
and I could not bear the idea of casting him upon
the parish. I therefore thank you, from my soul,
for affording me, as well as yourself, so pleasing a
gratification." I then desired to leave the entire
disposal of my young charge to him, only begging
that he would spare no proper expense to place
him in what situation he might think best, so as to
give him a chance of becoming a useful and respectable member of society. " To tell you the
truth," he replied, " I am anxious that he should,

if possible, remain, while he is yet so young, where
he now is, as I think he will not only receive
every care and attention himself, but he will also
be an object of interest to his protectresses, and
afford them a daily source of pleasure. Afterwards, if your benevolent views extend so far, it
appears to me, that he should be placed at some
respectable school, so as to be made capable, with
the assistance of his own labour and exertions, of
gaining his future livelihood. But we must think
farther on this matter, and, meanwhile, as you
seem to be at present what is called *an idle man,*
remember that my home and table will always be
honoured by your presence." After some further
conversation, I took my leave, with the happy
feeling glowing at my breast, that I had been enabled to do some little good to a forlorn fellow-
creature ; though, alas ! I also felt that our best
deeds of charity partake but too largely of the
frailty and imperfection of our nature, and that
their brightness is too often tarnished by a mixture
of weakness or of selfishness.

But if I proceed in my narration at this lag-
ing pace, I fear that my readers will discard me
as a fellow-traveller whose tediousness and pro-
lixity transform the minutes into hours, and the
miles into leagues. For my part, I own that I
love to wander over the fairy path which I trod at

this pleasing and happy period of my life,—to retrace every step,—and conjure up every charm which then captivated my heart and my fancy. But as I am aware that the loquacity of a lover (for such I soon became,) is seldom listened to with patience, I will hasten on with increased speed. Suffice it then to say, that the late events had given a new colouring to all my ideas. Instead of the weak invalid, seeking for health and amusement among the scenes and the beauties of nature, became a comparatively active being, endued with new life and spirits, invigorated by fresh hopes, animated by new desires. From this time, I was a frequent visitor at the parsonage, and a warm admirer of the worthy and excellent Mr. White, whose conversation partook at once of the scholar, the divine, and the man of the world. All that he said was deeply tinctured with that spirit of piety which influenced his actions, and the whole was seasoned with lively good humour and harmless raillery. His wife was a sensible domestic woman, who prized the talents, and revered the character of her husband, to whom she was a rational companion and willing help-mate. But I may, perhaps, hereafter, dwell more fully upon the peaceful inhabitants of this pretty but sequestered spot.

By the arguments and persuasions of Mr. White,

Mrs. Trevor was induced to shelter the little Edward under her roof, and, as his avowed protector, I of course frequently went to see my young protégé, and note his progress under the tender instruction of the amiable Louisa, to whom he became fondly attached, while his innocent prattle and engaging simplicity revived in the bosom of Mrs. Trevor feelings which had long lain dormant, but whose influence produced the most kindly effect upon a mind which had perhaps been too much sunk by the pressure of calamity.

Sometimes it was my good fortune to meet Louisa and her scholar rambling among the fields around the cottage, when the labours of the day were nearly completed, and the soft hue of twilight was succeeding to the full glare of day. Nor did she appear *greatly* to grieve at my approach, or to grudge me one of those sweet smiles of welcome which did not fail to set every pulse within my foolish heart in motion. The evenings were in general too inviting to permit us immediately to enter the cottage, and we generally contrived to get upon some topic so interesting to us both, that we forgot that the attractive mildness of the atmosphere was superseded by the damp air of night. I found that she was an unaffected admirer of poetry, and that her ideas of it were at once chaste, just, and glowing. I therefore sometimes brought

F

with me a favourite poet, or some good prose-writer, to wile away the morning hours while she was working indefatigably at her easel, and her mother was employed with equal industry at her needle.

All my fine resolves of absenting myself until the arrival of my father were forgotten; and, indeed, I had the vanity to believe that my daily visits were really acceptable. Interested as I could not disguise to myself my affections were gradually becoming in the lovely Louisa, I bent my whole attention upon her character, and scrutinized even her looks and actions; but, the first proceeding from the guileless simplicity of an amiable heart, and the latter dictated no less by the kindness of her feelings than the strength and excellence of her principles, could defy the minutest examination to discover any thing that was censurable. Her countenance was always free and undisguised,—her manners soft, pleasing, and entirely unaffected. Her conversation partook of the mind from which it flowed, being sometimes diversified with the light strains of easy gaiety, but more generally tinctured with the reflective cast which had been given to her thoughts by the melancholy scenes which she had been doomed to witness, and tinged with the deep nature of the feelings which warmed her bosom. As a daughter, she was indeed perfect. All her care, all her

thoughts, and all her labours, seemed to tend
towards mitigating the sorrows, or increasing the
comforts of her mother. All those little soothing
and delicate attentions which gratitude and affection suggest, were paid by her ; and any little personal sacrifice was made, not only willingly, but
with joy. I frequently found her engaged in
drawing, of which, she gave me to understand,
she was very fond; but I, who knew for what
purpose her pencil was so assiduously employed,
estimated her meritorious perseverance in its fullest
sense, and I had the silent but delightful satisfaction of purchasing from my friend the bookseller
several of her pieces, for which I could thus give
the equivalent which their excellence demanded,
but perhaps might not always procure ; and on
these pictures would I gaze with rapture, while I
thought I could perceive the fair hand of this
virtuous daughter tracing each line in the service
of her scarcely less estimable mother. The time
which was not devoted to this primary object, she
seemed to employ in improving her mind by the
perusal of their small but well-assorted library of
books, or in performing all those quiet and domestic duties, the proper fulfilment of which constitutes one of the principal duties of a female, while
it adds an additional charm to her character; or
else in visiting a few of the poor cottagers around,

to whom she liberally rendered every assistance which it was in her limited power to bestow. They called her the " good young lady of the white cottage;" and often did I listen with silent delight to the high but deserved praises which they so liberally lavished upon her. These circumstances, as well as all those numerous but beautiful shades which tell the history of the mind, were of course developed by degrees, and the farther I advanced in hers, the more I discovered to admire and to love. She possessed, too, a nobleness, an elevation of soul, the want of which I have found frequent cause to regret in the softer sex, at the same time that she had all the mildness and the delicacy which is, perhaps, their most attractive charm. To this also was added, that without which every attraction is fleeting, every good quality insecure—she had a strong sense of the awful truths of *religion ;* and her every action was impressed by this belief, and guided by this feeling. There was no boasted goodness, no parade of piety ; her's was evidently that firm and settled devotion which imperceptibly actuates every deed, and spontaneously shines forth upon every emergency, which is always awake and upon the watch, but is never exhibited foolishly or unreasonably.

One evening, on returning to my inn, I observed a chaise standing before the door, from which the

horses were just being led by the landlord, who
performed also the part of hostler; but, occupied by
my own thoughts, I did not inquire into the cause
of so unusual an event as the arrival of strangers
at this secluded place, but proceeded to my own
apartment, where, on opening the door, I observed
a gentleman standing with his back towards me;
but the air, the contour of the figure, was enough;
it was my father, and I sprung forwards, and was
in an instant pressed to his warm and paternal
bosom. Oh! what a golden tie is that which binds
together the parent and the child! It is unstained
by vice, untarnished by selfishness, unsullied by
vanity; for gratitude forms its imperishable basis,
and the glow of pure affection polishes and brightens its surface. Its links are fastened into the inmost recesses of the heart, and are severed by
death, only to be more firmly re-united in the
mansions of eternity!

When the first interchange of affection was over,
and just as I was going to inquire after the health
of my beloved mother and sisters, I felt some one
tap me on my cheek, and in the same instant beheld
my little blooming Phœbe standing gaily before me.
She had concealed herself behind the door, and
silently enjoyed the interview between my father
and myself. "What! so you will not see ' puss
in the corner,' will you? or," added she, putting

on one of her most playful looks, " or are your powers of sight so weakened by gazing on the dazzling effulgence of this wood-nymph you have lately discovered, that they are now circumscribed to her alone, and unable to behold the un-etherial form of your common-place sister ? Bless me, brother ! why I've actually brought the ruddy tinge of modesty into your manly cheek,—and my dear father, do but look at him ! I protest, the sweets and beauties of this said paradise have given him a new existence. The balmy zephyrs of this Elysian grove have brought back the look and animation of health ; or has the fair one who presides there," continued she, laughing, " wooed it back with her soft glances ?" Thus she went rattling on for some time, until she had dissipated the foolish embarrassment which she had caused in my tell-tale countenance ; and we then entered into a conversation, the sweets of which can only be felt by those who have met with friends whom they love, and from whom they have been some time separated. While my sister was surveying the apartments assigned to her, I confessed to my father that I felt a growing attachment for Louisa, and that from my knowledge of his principles and his kindness I did not doubt his approving of my choice. I then described her character and conduct, and expatiated on her very superior endowments of

mind and person; " but however, my dear father,"
I added, " you must see her to do her justice—you
must"——" Ah, ah, no doubt," exclaimed Phœbe,
as she at this moment tripped into the room, " a
lover's pencil, you know, is always dipped in the
most sombre tints of nature. But I must positively see this ' fair excellence ' myself, and judge
with my own clear and unbiassed optics, and so
Frederic, when shall we storm this pretty cottage
of hers ?" This question was answered by our
unanimously agreeing to walk to Mrs. Trevor's the
following morning; and I looked forward with the
greatest pleasure to introducing Phœbe and Louisa
to each other. The day seemed to smile upon my
wishes; it was indeed a lovely morning, and we set
off with great glee to pay our intended visit. Mrs.
Trevor and Louisa were engaged in their usual
occupations, and the little Edward was reading to
them his morning lesson. My father and his old
friend met each other with the most cordial pleasure, and Phœbe and Miss Trevor seemed to be
drawn together by an irresistible attraction, for in
the short space of half an hour they appeared as
much at their ease as if they had been long acquainted. In fine, we spent one of those mornings
to which the heart recurs with fond remembrance,
and on which it can dwell with calm and unruffled
pleasure, and at length took our leave with great

and visible reluctance. " Well," said my father,
after a few minutes conversation, " but you do not
tell us, Phœbe, whether or not you have detected
any errors in the lover's portrait." " Why, to tell
you the truth," she replied, " the little mischievous
god has I believe actually placed the bandage before *my* eyes, for I cannot yet find a single thing in
this all-perfect fair one with which to find fault,
and I begin to hope that her heart is made of such
very soft materials, that Frederic may mould it into
his own likeness. By the way, I do not think that
she absolutely hates you, brother, or else her eyes
and cheeks tell tales about nothing." " My dear
sister!" exclaimed I, seizing her hand, " My dear
Phœbe, do you really think that she loves me—that
she—that if— tat I may—" " That she—that if
—that I may.—Plain and reasonable questions, to
which I will answer with due form and precision.
First, that she—which I translate, ' is in love?'
Why, I think Cupid is now resolutely besieging her
heart, and he will, if I mistake not, very speedily
carry it by storm. Let me see, what is the second
query ?—that if ? which, added to the third—that I
may ? I construe thus—' that if I fall down on my
knees before her angelic form, and swear that I value
her even more than my own sweet self, will she be
sapient enough to give me credit, and to trust to the
declarations of selfish inconstant man ?' Why, in

real verity, I believe she is just now a *very woman*, with her heart melted to such a feminine softness, that the silvery tones of love will glide smoothly into its deepest recesses. At any rate, my dear brother, remember the old saying, that ' faint heart never won fair lady;' and if you intend to *capture* this lovely prize, you must not approach her with *drooping colours*. Be bold, and I in prophetic language pronounce that you will be fortunate."

I resolved to follow my sister's advice, and to take the first opportunity of declaring my affection to Louisa. But day after day passed away, and found me still a silent, although an adoring lover. I dreaded to dispel the pleasing illusion by discovering that I loved alone; and I could not persuade myself to risk the loss of society which formed the chief happiness of my existence. My sister frequently rallied me on my cowardice of heart, as she provokingly termed it, but even her raillery might have been for some time unavailing in restoring my confidence, had not an unexpected incident forced from me the declaration which I wished, yet dreaded to make.

One eventful day, I accompanied my father and Phœbe to the cottage. Mrs. Trevor was alone in her little garden, enjoying the beauty of a clear, bright evening, and she informed us that Louisa was a little indisposed, and had therefore remained within. On hearing this, I quickly hastened to find her, forgetting, at the moment, any thing but the impulse which impelled me forwards. The object of my search was sitting by an open window; she held a paper in her hand, on which her tears were fast flowing. I softly approached her, but she was too much absorbed in her own meditations immediately to hear or to perceive me. " Yes," she muttered, again looking at the paper on which I perceived was a little poem which I had some time before transcribed for her. " Yes, I feel I do indeed love thee, but shall this feeling, this weakness"— " Oh! call it not a weakness," I exclaimed, rushing forwards and throwing myself at her feet, " call it not a weakness, my beloved Louisa! tell me, O tell me, am I indeed so blessed? Is it me—*me*, that you really love?" My impetuous manner, and passionate gestures, recalled her to herself, for she at first seemed stunned by my unexpected appearance. Her self-possession, however, strengthened as it was by principle, soon returned to her. With cheeks suffused with blushes, and in a manner struggling between emotion and a sense of dignity, she said, " After what you have just heard, it is in vain for me to deny how much I—I—esteem you. Nor can I hope that you will forget my indiscretion; but I entreat, I implore you to consider the worse than folly I have displayed, as the result of a momentary weakness, for which I shall never forgive myself. I beseech you, let me go, for I have lowered myself sufficiently in my own eyes, without farther degrading myself in yours." She uttered these words in a tone of such deep mortification as pierced me to the heart, and I hastened to appease her wounded delicacy, by reproaching her for desiring to leave me when I had so long waited but an opportunity of declaring my love. I then confessed to her all my feelings and my hopes, and pressed my suit with the earnestness of true affection. " I have not," added I, " riches to offer you,—but they would not win your affection; I have not rank to bestow,—but that would not dazzle your eyes; and if independence with a man who admires, who adores you—Oh! Louisa! what is it that should divide us?" She looked gratified, soothed; while a gleam of happiness passed over her tearful countenance. But again shrinking, as if at some sudden thought, and then summoning with evident effort an air of resolution, " Yes," she said, " there *is* cause to divide us. I cannot deny that my heart is yours; but to indulge the feelings of that heart, you shall not have to present a portionless bride to your family. You shall not have hereafter to repent that your youthful enthusiasm led you to sacrifice your future prospects in the world. No—may you

—may you be happy with some other than Louisa." When she had whispered, rather then pronounced, the last words, and was rising to depart, I vehemently exclaimed, " Never, never, Louisa, will I wed any one but you !—never can I give my heart to any other ! and would you," continued I, with a reproachful look, " when I ask your love, tell me that you have not *gold?* No, dearest, this is only the scruple of an over delicate mind. My father loves you, and will be proud to own you as his daughter; my mother is already prepared to bless you as her own ; and yours, Louisa, yours, shall not lose the tender prop which has so long sustained her. She shall hallow our union with her presence, and our home with her society." " Oh, Frederic !" (it was the first time she had thus addressed me, and I secretly blessed the auspicious omen,) " what a beautiful prospect you present to me—yet it cannot be—it *surely* cannot be"——— " And why can it not be, Louisa ? Nothing but yourself can prevent it, and if you indeed love me"———" If," repeated she, softly, casting her eyes upon the ground, but instantly raising them and making a sudden start : surprised at this movement, I followed her glance, and beheld my father just entering from the garden. I instantly led Louisa to him. " My dear father," said I, " your son is blessed beyond his hope ; he has won this precious gem——" " Then wear it, my son, in thy heart's core," replied he, placing Louisa's hand in mine, " and may a parent's blessing diminish not its value in thy estimation." At this moment, Mrs. Trevor and Phœbe entered; I hastened to the former, and besought her consent to my promised happiness, which she gave me in terms which completed my satisfaction, while tears of joy and tenderness streamed down her aged cheeks. A scene of delight which in the short time of human existence is not allowed often to take place, succeeded, and although quickly carried away by the rapid stream of time, its impression yet remains upon my mind, and is firmly engraven upon the tablet of memory.

The hours now glided on in so smooth and pleasing a course, that I was not even sensible of their progress. Much of our time was spent in discussing my future plans. It was agreed that I should fix my residence on a little estate belonging to my family, and situated at no great distance from the paternal mansion; and that Mrs. Trevor, who could ill dispense with the attentions which she had been accustomed to receive from Louisa, should continue to reside with her; that I should return home, and prepare every thing for the speedy solemnization of our nuptials, and that Mr. White should join us in the happy bands of Hymen! I

must not omit to mention that my father had conceived a great respect and friendship for that excellent old man, and he cordially invited both himself
and his family to visit him.

The day of departure at length arrived, and I
felt it as one of severe trial ; for I could not leave
without regret, even for a short period, the scenes
in which I had experienced so much pleasure, and
which were therefore endeared to me no less by the
thousand sweet recollections that they excited, than
by the treasured form which still existed amongst
them. " God bless thee, my Louisa !" said I,
clasping her to my breast, " soon will thy happy
Frederic return to claim this loved hand, and make
thee all his own !" and then bursting away, I hurried back to the inn, threw myself into the chaise
with my father and sister, and was soon far from
the spot which contained what I most prized upon
earth.

Spurred on by the impatience of love, I had
soon made every necessary arrangement, and having
engaged that my whole family should follow me in
a few days, and bless my nuptials with their presence, I set off on my return to the abode of my
Louisa, every moment seeming to me an age that
detained me from her. The instant that I again
descended at the *White Hart*, I sprung out of the
carriage, and in spite of the earnest entreaties of

my officious landlady that I would take some refreshment after my journey, set off full speed for
the White Cottage. As I paced each well-known
field with hasty steps, I remembered the first time
that I had crossed them in the same direction, and
thought over my discovery of the virtuous Louisa,
and every subsequent incident which marked our
acquaintance. "And thou art going to be mine!"
I mentally exclaimed, with the rapturous feelings
of a lover, "and the virtues which thou hast displayed in the hours of poverty and adversity, shall
never be forgotten by thy Frederic." High beat
my heart as I caught the first glimpse of the
cottage peeping through the trees, and when I had
passed the last field, and stood before the little gate
which opened into the garden, every pulse in my
bosom throbbed with the eagerness of expectation.
But it was only the exaltation of a moment; like
the lightning's glare, which by the powers of contrast serves to render a scene of desolation but the
more appalling; for in the next, I beheld the
cottage closed up in every part, and evidently unin-
habited, or inhabited by mourners. A thrill of
horror shot through my veins, and a damp chill
spread over my heart, as I thought of the possibility of the latter being the case, and for a minute
or two I was unable to stir from the spot in which
I was. With desperate courage, however, I rushed

to the door and essayed to open it, but it resisted
every effort.   I rapped, but no one answered to my
call, and though I repeated my summons, all was
silent.   I tried the windows, but all were fast, and
in an agony of mind greater than I can describe, I
called upon the names of Louisa and Mrs. Trevor,
and paced with frantic steps before the cottage.   A
short time, however, brought me to reflection, and
collecting my scattered thoughts, I endeavoured to
think of something which might account for this
inexplicable desertion.   I felt sure that Mrs. Trevor could not be gone to any of her friends, because I knew her wish of concealing from them as
much as possible her place of residence ; and I had
besides, received a letter from Louisa two days before, in which no intention of the kind was even
hinted at.   What, then, was I to suppose ?   Here
a thought darted like fire through my brain, that
Sir Edward Stanley might have ensnared away my
bride, and that her mother might be gone in search
of her.   The idea was horrible, and unable to sustain it longer, I determined to return to the village
and employ every means for the discovery of the
truth.   I had, however, only proceeded about a
hundred yards, when I to my infinite joy descried
the welcome form of my friend Peggy advancing
towards me, and hastening to her, I overwhelmed
her with innumerable inquiries.   At first the poor

girl seemed quite confounded by my vehemence,
but quickly recovering herself, she said, " Oh!
Sir, then you have not heard my poor mistress"——
" What of your mistress, in the name of Heaven,"
I exclaimed, " tell me."

" Why, Sir, she has been taken to gaol by some
rascal of a lawyer, though she promised to pay
him what she owed him in a very short time ; and
Miss Louisa is gone with her, Sir, and I am left
to take care of the cottage, and so, as I was
obliged to go to the village, I shut it quite up before I left."

" And when did all this take place," said I,
endeavouring to assume an appearance of calmness
which I was far from possessing. " Only yesterday, Sir ; and Miss Louisa, before she went, wrote
a letter to you, Sir, which I afterwards sent, and
may be,——that is, I'm sure she'd be very glad to
see you." " But where is she ?" replied I, starting at this suggestion, and almost relieved to find
that my fears of my rival's nefarious arts having
been employed were false, " where can I find
her ?" This, and every other information which I
could, I gained from my simple companion, and
then charging her to let no one know what had
passed, I hurried on resolved to proceed immediately to the neighbouring town where the prison
was situated. Accordingly, I mounted my horse

G

in all haste, to the no small surprise and conster-
nation of my faithful John, who, however, insisted
upon accompanying me, fearing, as he said, " that
I should over-do myself." It was late when I arrived at the place of my destination, and I was
obliged to give up all idea of seeing that night the
objects of my search. Heavy then appeared to me
the wings of time, but at length " welcome morn"
arrived, and even before the hour of admittance
was come, I found myself at the gate of the miserable habitation which contained her who was dearest to me upon earth, and as I gazed upon its
gloomy walls, I could scarcely refrain from exe-
crating the wretch who had immured her within
them.

A surly porter appeared at my summons, and
ushered me into a court, where the unfortunate
debtors were allowed to breathe awhile the air of
heaven. Here another man appeared, and led me
to a door which he opened, and I found myself in
the presence of Louisa and her mother. With an
accent of mingled surprise and joy, the former
started from her seat. Then, as if some painful
feeling passed across her breast to damp its more
pleasing emotions, she put her hand over her eyes,
and sunk again into her chair. " Louisa, my own
Louisa," I exclaimed, perfectly comprehending
the cause of this involuntary motion, " will you

not greet your Frederic ?" and I clasped her to a
heart where her image was so fondly enshrined.

" Oh, Frederic," she faintly uttered, " what a
place to meet your destined wife! and can you
accept a bride who has been thus disgraced in the
eye of the world ?"

" Disgraced, Louisa! you never looked to me
more lovely than at this instant, and in this
wretched place."

So absorbing are the feelings of love, that I
had scarcely until this moment discerned Mrs. Trevor, to whom, however, I now addressed myself,
and from whom I besought an explanation of the
almost inexplicable events which had taken place,
and from her lips I received the following account.

After the death of her husband, she had been
compelled to employ a professional man on several
occasions, to transact her affairs, and she had se-
lected one who was generally considered to be
guided by feelings of humanity, as well as by
principles of justice and integrity. The debt
which she thus necessarily contracted, she was
rendered unable to pay, but she agreed to dis-
charge it by small instalments as she could save
for that purpose from her scanty pittance, and she
had hitherto done so at stated periods, without
receiving any complaint. " Two days ago, however," added she, " some men arrived at the cot-

and holding out to him the promise of a handsome reward if he complied with my desire. At this welcome conclusion of my harangue, his grim features relaxed somewhat of their sternness, and a watery smile even passed over them as he informed me that " another young gentleman" had been inquiring for the ladies while I was with them; but, on hearing they were engaged with me, had abruptly departed, desiring him not to speak of his visit. I asked him if he knew where this gentleman was to be found. " Why, Sir," he replied, " I was going along the street soon after he had been here, and I saw him coming out of an inn, paying the hostler, and getting into a gig, in which he drove away, so that I suppose he is gone altogether." A piece of money rewarded this information, and, having received a much lower bow at departing than I had been favoured with at entering, from my sordid conductor, I hastened to my inn, resolved to lose no time in seeking for one so contemptible as Sir Edward Stanley, and who was so evidently bent on avoiding me ; but rather to obtain the immediate release of the objects of his persecution. Leaving a note for John to deliver with his own hands to Louisa, in which I expressed a hope of escorting her out of their uncomfortable mansion on the following morning, and promising, at any rate, to be with her, I set off for the residence of the lawyer, full of the hope of restoring my beloved Louisa and her mother to liberty.

I will not fatigue the reader with any account of my interview with this man. I will only say, that I obtained from him all that I desired,—namely, an order for the release of Mrs. Trevor, and with this valuable accompaniment I found myself next day again at the doors of the prison. In a few moments I was admitted, but I needed not to tell my tale—Louisa read my errand in my countenance, and Oh! how sweetly did I feel myself repaid by the glance of grateful and confiding tenderness which she cast upon me. Without speaking, she pressed my hand, and turned from me to conceal the tears which were trembling in her eyes ; the pressure was rapturously returned : and thus, without the articulation of a syllable, did we, by the talismanic influence of love, behold the feelings of each other's heart.

It would be tedious to narrate every little circumstance that ensued. Suffice it to say, that the following day again saw Mrs. Trevor and Louisa the inhabitants of the *White Cottage,* and my parents, sisters, and myself, the lodgers of my " gracious hostess" of the *White Hart.* My family had arrived on the preceding evening, and, unable to gather any explicit account of what had passed, were in the greatest perplexity and distress.

Now, however, all was happy and serene; and the day which was to consummate my happiness arrived clear and unclouded as my own felicity. I tasted of the cup of joy gladly, though with trembling, and Heaven, in its mercy, dashed it not away, but granted me as large a portion as man is allowed, or is capable of enjoying.

The enthusiasm of *that* hour has passed away. The airy visions of the ardent lover, who would enshrine his mistress in the mould of perfection, are flown; but, being raised not merely by passion, but by esteem and reverence, they have not been succeeded by satiety or disgust, but by a milder and therefore more durable affection, and by a calm consciousness of domestic happiness, which constitutes the summit of earthly bliss, and strews the path of life with sweets and flowers.

And now, having I doubt not established my character with the reader of a prosing egotistical fellow, I will, at any rate, in the overflowings of my benevolence, add a few words in his, to the many I have employed in my own service. In the first place, then, my good friend, as I am now arriving at an age which pretends to wisdom, if it does not possess it, let me advise you, if you are (what I was once) ardent and susceptible, and untroubled with any cumbrous load of prudence or caution, never to let any *beautiful incognita* seize upon your heart, for although, as I have narrated, the goddess of my fancy proved afterwards the choice of my reason also, I am yet ready to acknowledge that for this happy circumstance I am more indebted to a fortunate chance, than owe it to my own discretion or circumspection, and I am aware that when the imagination is allowed to lead, common sense halts sadly in the rear, and is seldom ready to quicken its pace, and advance to the assistance of its possessor when most it is needed. Secondly, having for some years experienced the blessings of the connubial state, I would, with all due deference, recommend to him who belongeth to the right primitive and respectable class of *old bachelors*, to take a friendly hint, and turn in his mind the possibility of making an interest in the breast of some warm-hearted spinster, (before the gout ties him to his elbow-chair, or that archenemy time wrinkles his forehead,) who will occupy the vacant nook in his chimney-corner,—enliven his empty sitting-room,—minister to him when he is sick,—soothe him when he is sorrowful,—and smile upon him when he is joyful. Thirdly, that my sage counsel may stand some small chance of being weighed as it deserves in the scale of calm deliberation, I must add a few words in my own justification ; for what man will attend to the advice of one whom he regards as cherishing silly and romantic ideas unbecoming the gravity of his age, and the professed gravity of his advice ? But alas! even the wisest of us, it is said, have their weak moments, and I confess some of mine to have been employed in the vain occupation of retracing the triumphs of my youth, and dwelling complacently upon them, until I again have fancied myself the ardent lover, and the vigorous young man, and used a language becoming to characters so little philosophic. I assure you, however, gentle reader, that excepting when the vagaries of my youth flash across me for a few moments, I am as sober an old fellow as you can desire, and fully entitled to your reverent attention; and this declaration, when proceeding from so high a quarter, I feel convinced you will not be inclined to dispute.

As I flatter myself that I have sufficiently interested you in my youthful fortunes, to make you desirous of knowing those of my maturer age, I will add a few words of the present situation of my family, and the events which have taken place in this lapse of years, that having made you acquainted with my character and pretensions, I may hope as a return, that you will pay some attention to my valuable lucubrations.

Blessed with the sight of mine and of her daughter's happiness, Mrs. Trevor soon forgot the disgust which she had conceived of the world, and the feelings of wounded pride which she had nourished. Her benevolent spirit again shone forth to cheer the landscape of life both to herself, and to those who were around her. She lived to see Louisa the happy mother of three blooming children; and having spent her latter years in peace, her spirit fled from earth, to join, we dare to hope, the communion of saints in heaven.

Although, however, she was almost our constant inmate, she was still the ostensible inhabitant of the White Cottage, which I purchased as a memorial of my happiness, and which she rented from me.

Her persecutor, Sir Edward Stanley, after spending a few years in dissipation of almost every kind, was killed by a fall from his horse, and thus hurried into eternity with all his sins unrepented of and unexpiated.

My father, " ripe in virtue and good deeds," has also finished his course. But my mother still remains amongst us, and lives with my " little Phœbe," now a fine commanding woman, whose ardent nature, mellowed by a disappointment which she was doomed to experience, and whose warm heart, unsoured by its wound, is now exercised for her friends, in whose service she is zealous and indefatigable, and to whom she is at once a comfort and a delight. Caroline is united to a

worthy and amiable man, and by her numerous
excellencies continues to raise the esteem, and en-
dear to her the hearts of all with whom she is connected : and I—but I will describe the scene at
this moment before my eyes, which will give a
complete idea of my immediate situation without
farther prelude.

Before me sits a female whose mild and intelligent countenance is formed to charm the eye of
the beholder, whose serene and open forehead
speaks a mind at peace with itself, and whose still
fine features tell the tale of former loveliness.   She
is instructing a little girl who stands beside her,
and in whom I acknowledge my little Emma.   The
reader will, I hope, recognise in this portrait the
Louisa of my youthful preference, still the Louisa
of my warmest affections.   A little farther, I see
a curly-headed youth, and a smiling girl, engaged
in some innocent sport; and, seated still farther,
by themselves, I every now and then venture to
take a peep at a fine young man, with a frank military air, and an honest and expressive countenance,
who seems to be impressing some very earnest and
important truth on the ear of a blushing maiden,
who, with downcast eyes, but not ungratified looks,
is listening to the momentous words.   These two
are my protégé Edward and my eldest daughter,
who bears not only the name but the lineaments of

her mother. So much was the former endeared to us by his helpless situation, as well as by the sweetness of his disposition, and the attachment he manifested to us both, that we agreed to bring him up as our own child; and never have we had cause to repent this indulgence of our feelings. Noble, brave, and fearless, perhaps almost to excess, he possesses also strong principles, and a tender heart, and, despising every thing approaching to meanness in others, is himself candid and generous. The infant Louisa was his favourite plaything, and she was yet a child, when impelled by martial ardour, he entered the army. When he returned to us in the course of a few years, with his fine figure ripened into manly beauty, and his countenance lighted up with the consciousness of having obtained deserved applause, she was shooting up into the blooming woman, with her embryo charms just disclosing themselves to view. No wonder then, that infantine love was exchanged for a warmer attachment. No wonder that her " dear brother Edward" became soon possessed of a still stronger interest in her heart; or that the before " little Louisa" became the chosen of his ——.

My wife and myself beheld the gradual change of sentiment, nor did it in any way alarm us. We had long carefully studied the character of our adopted son, and we felt that it was one calcu-

lated to make the life of our daughter happy.
True, his origin was mean, his parentage ignoble,
but we felt that virtue is more precious than the
one, and happiness of far more value than the
other. We, therefore, rather encouraged than repressed the partiality which we saw growing between them, and which speedily ripened into the
fondest affection. As soon as Edward was conscious of the nature of his feelings, he openly acknowledged them to me, declared his resolution of
sacrificing them to his duty and his gratitude, and
his desire of immediately departing to his regiment.
" No, my son," I replied, " I did not save you
from poverty, to inflict on you a still more grievous
wound. You are worthy of Louisa. I believe she
loves you, or if not," I added, smiling, " perhaps
you may be able to discover some road to her affections." Equally astonished and enraptured, he
uttered the most vehement expressions of gratitude ; and soon afterwards told his tale of love,
and was not rejected. Louisa, however, is yet
young, and as Edward's leave of absence is almost
expired, he is to return again to claim his youthful
bride, whose heart now pants at the dread of her
lover's danger, now springs with hope at the idea
of his speedily coming back to her unchanged in
heart, and perhaps crowned with laurels.

Such then has been my lot. But I must add,

that although the picture I have drawn be fair and
smiling, I have yet, like the rest of my fellow-
mortals, experienced many of the troubles and
perplexities of this sublunary world : and, though
I may have drank of the cup of joy, I am not unacquainted with the bitterness of sorrow. What I
would remark, therefore, is, that the *means* of attaining happiness are pretty equally divided among
the sons of men, although they may be greatly
increased or diminished by themselves ; for, to a
contented mind, every state appears with its own
peculiar charms ; and to a murmuring and repining
spirit, the brightest gifts of nature, or fortune, are
vain and useless.

Reader ! whatever be thy situation in life, be
sure thou hast much more than thou deservest—
much more than thou canst pretend to claim.
Bend, therefore, with resignation, under the rod
which may be sometimes sent to chasten thee, and
enjoy, with a thankful and confiding heart, the
good which may graciously be allotted thee—

> Content and grateful, be thy well-pois'd mind,
> By joy, unspoiled,—in misery, resigned.

REFLECTIONS.

Through Nature's ample range I hold my course,
Gaze on its beauties, contemplate their source.

I BELIEVE I am naturally of a contemplative turn
of mind; and therefore, when many of those
around me are seeking amusement from the passing events of life, I retire as it were into myself,
and become wrapt up in my own meditations.
Now, to a man of this disposition, nature affords
ample and never-failing sources of delight, and
produces unceasing subjects for reflection. Where-
ever he turns, he finds something to excite his curiosity, and to rouse his spirit of inquiry; and in
this wide and varied field he can wander with an
unsatiated mind, and an unwearied eye. As no
study can be more entertaining, so none is so pure,
or so instructive. It is one that tends to exalt and
elevate the soul, to soothe and subdue the passions,
and to improve the heart. It is not only the delight of the poet, the painter, and the man of feeling, but is one of the highest enjoyments of the

Christian. By the latter, indeed, only are all its sweet but hidden charms discovered. He descries a thousand beauties which those who are not under the influence of his great and enlightened feelings, can never penetrate. He alone feels truly their effect upon his heart, although they may charm the fancy of enthusiasm, gratify the eye of taste, or rouse the mind of philosophy. I confess that it seems to me truly extraordinary that any one can survey at all the grand and beautiful features of Nature, without being drawn to the contemplation of " Nature's God;" nor can I conceive how the soul can rest satisfied with admiring the creature, without dwelling on the far sublimer idea of the Creator, except by supposing that it dreads that painful feeling of humiliation which must accompany the thought of a Being so far above the comprehension of finite man.

Often, indeed, when I have gazed upon the rich canopy of heaven, beheld the numberless stars which seem to sparkle on its surface, and the lovely moon, which sheds her modest light upon the softened landscape ; or the more brilliant luminary who darts his piercing rays upon every object, and covers the earth with the radiance of his glory—I have been overwhelmed with a feeling of inexpressible astonishment, mingled with a strong sensation of awe, and in *that moment*, even painfully

H

alive to my own littleness, I have been tempted to
exclaim, "What," indeed, "*is* man, that thou art
mindful of him, or the son of man that thou re-
gardest him!" The idea has rushed on my mind,
"What am I, amid this scene of wonders? In the
immense globe which I inhabit, I am but as a grain
of sand upon the sea-shore, which is dispersed by
the winds of heaven;" and when I have considered
that thousands of other worlds exist, to whom our
globe is but as the little stars which we see dazzling
in the firmament, I have shrunk at my own insigni-
ficance, and felt a momentary dread that I should
be lost and overlooked in the immensity of creation.
But from this painful feeling, this dreadfully-de-
pressing idea, I have quickly returned to a joyful
sense of the merciful and omnipresent nature of the
Deity; and in the transporting assurance that he
will never leave, never forsake, his children, I have
raised up my grateful soul in silent, heart-felt adoration.

If an entire conviction of this truth did not, indeed, result from the evidences of Scripture, yet a
view of nature itself would completely evince its
reality; for although some few of its features may
be calculated to excite principally emotions of awe
and wonder, the greater number raise those of
pleasing admiration; and the whole comprehended
together, create in the heart the warmest sentiments

of grateful piety; so that while we view the careful
Father, the gracious God, which are displayed so
fully throughout the universe, we feel a happy
trust that there *is* surely a kind hand which shields
us from evil, and directs every incident of our lives.
Is there *one* link in the vast chain of creation,
which is not directed by his providence? Does it
appear that one part is left to govern itself, or influence its own actions? The universal and unerring
voice of Nature proclaims that it does *not;* and
from the heavens which surround us, to the mean-
est insect, and the leaf on which it dwells, all declare a wise and all powerful God, who, as a tender
Father, continually preserves and protects all things
which he has formed into being.

Confined, however, as we are to the small space
which is allotted for our movements upon earth, we
find it difficult to believe that nothing can bound
the view of the Almighty; and narrow as are our
own conceptions, and circumscribed our limits, we
cannot imagine a Being who fills infinite space with
his presence, and possesses infinite, unbounded
knowledge. But it is the certainty of this omni-
presence and omniscience of God, which makes us
feel so sure of his constant protection, and gives us
that unspeakable comfort in the hour of affliction;
that he sees all our motions, knows every thing that

happens to us, and therefore that all is wisely ordered for the best.

But imperfect as our ideas are of the attributes
of God, and of the perfection of his nature, our
notions are still sufficiently extended to enable us to
contemplate in some measure the great Being
whom we are taught to reverence and adore; and
our reason tells us that he possesses qualities far
superior to those which we annex to his nature, as
our conceptions must be bounded to those virtues
alone which ourselves are enabled to possess; or to
use the expressive words of Addison, " As he has
in him all the perfection of a spiritual nature, and
since we have no notion of any kind of spiritual perfection but what we discover in our own souls, we
join infinitude to each kind of these perfections, and
what is a faculty in a human soul, becomes an
attribute in God."

What a subject of astonishment is it that man,
insignificant as he is, should be so frequently
buoyed up with an idea of his own wisdom and
power; that vanity should feed on his brain, and
pride contaminate his heart. Can we conceive a
conduct more truly absurd than to value ourselves
on gifts which are gratuitously bestowed on us, by
a bountiful Providence ! Are we blessed with a
lovely or prepossessing exterior? Let us reflect

whose hand formed the noble structure, and moulded it from the dust. Are we rich in the graces of
a lively imagination, or endued with a vigorous understanding? Who infused the breath of life into
the creature which he had made, and blessed it
with a soul to animate the clay of which it consisted? If, added to these natural blessings which
are granted us, we be crowned with health, surrounded by riches and honours, or raised, even by
our own merit, to the pinnacle of fame; does not
the same kind Being protect the frail substance he
raised out of the dust, and preserve its various
parts in their due place and order, regulating every
tender fibre, and tuning every susceptible nerve
with careful tenderness? Is not the same goodness
visible in every blessing which attends us? And is
not our very virtue itself sustained by his spirit,
and supported by his merciful protection? Were
he not every moment to guard and defend us, how
soon should we fall into the snares that are laid for
us! How soon would our weak faith be overcome,
our boasted virtue vanish.

I feel that all know, all will acknowledge this;
but, as an excellent authoress of the present age
(whose fine pen has been employed, and successfully employed, in inculcating the sublime truths
of religion, and diffusing through her country a
higher admiration of virtue,) declares, " The world

requires more to be reminded than informed," and therefore such truths cannot be too frequently, or too strongly, presented to the mind, until the fruits of our knowledge be more constantly displayed in our lives and actions.

But were we not convinced of our utter dependance on the Almighty, and that all is directed by, and proceeds from, his infinite wisdom, the very consciousness of the instability of our possessions ought to subdue every feeling of vanity, every emotion of pride. Let us look around us, and behold the beauteous form, and engaging countenance, defaced by accident or disease, or destroyed by the ruthless hand of unpitying Death. Let us see the intelligence and vivacity of a mind replete with every grace, and rich in every branch of useful knowledge, sinking under the pressure of bodily infirmities—perhaps, as a fierce and dazzling blaze, exhausted by its own brightness, and, like the famous bird of old, consumed by the very materials which it had itself collected and prepared. Behold, too, the boasted pile of wealth, sunk by some unexpected misfortune, or the pride of honours crushed by the breath of slander, or the whispers of malice. See the fickle goddess, Fame, changing every day the objects of her preference, and only placing the courted wreath on the brow of her favourite, to let him taste the insufficiency of her power to bestow the happiness he sought; or to desert him in the moment of triumph and exaltation, for some equally deluded object of her choice.

Oh man! frail and powerless as thou art, how can pride possess thine erring heart, or vanity destroy the beauty of thy mind? Son of the dust! soon shall thy frail body return to its mother earth, and thy boasted strength be laid low.

As nothing tends so much to inspire a spirit of true humility as such considerations as these, so scarcely any thing can warm the heart with such emotions of piety, as a frequent contemplation of the works of the Creator, displayed in the beauties of nature, and the formation of man. Astonished at the greatness of the design, as well as the finished regularity of its execution, our ideas are naturally raised from surveying the richness and grandeur of the workmanship, to the great Artificer who formed, designed, and completed it; and then, surely there is no heart so callous as not to feel a sentiment of gratitude mingle in the varied feelings which inspire it. Can we behold this goodly temple of our bodies,—survey with what wonderful nicety each part is adapted to its especial use, and all fitted for each other, how exactly they answer the calls and necessities of nature, and with what wondrous skill the whole is managed and contrived,—and not feel thankful, *sincerely thankful*, to the kind Being who blessed us with such a frame? Can we see the earth covered with fertility, and abounding in hidden and inexhaustible stores,—admire the stately tree of the forest, or the scarcely less useful herb which furnishes us with wholesome nourishment——or survey the number and variety of creatures formed for our special use,—and not bless the hand which has thus abundantly dispensed every blessing, and from which flows every good which we can either desire or enjoy? Can we, I repeat, reflect on all these mercies, and return from the examination without one touch of grateful transport, one throb of grateful piety? No, surely; that heart must be callous indeed to every virtuous sentiment, which will not at such a time confess and feel, that our God is indeed a " God of mercy."

I may, I think, conclude, then, by finally observing, that the study of nature, both animate and inanimate, must be extremely beneficial to the mind. It must insensibly raise a higher strain of feeling, and a purer course of habitual thought. It must soften the asperities, and reduce the inordinate pride of man; and it must gradually draw him closer to the great Father of all, by which alone he can enjoy true comfort here, or happiness hereafter. Infinite, indeed, must be that goodness which condescends to lead him towards himself, through the medium of attractions so innocent, but so sublime.

> " Not content
> With every food of life to nourish man
> By kind illusions of the wond'ring sense,
> *It* makes all nature beauty to his eye,
> Or music to his ear."

FOND MEMORIALS.

Death! thou may'st break the thread of life
That knit me to my friend. But still will Memory
Be busy in this heart; and still my soul
Will cherish the lov'd form thou hast destroy'd,
And hang upon the accents thou hast still'd;
While each fond token, each memento sweet
Of my lost treasure, and my fleeting bliss,
I'll guard with melancholy joy

THERE is something irresistibly touching and beautiful in the tender mementos which are in some places nourished of those whose spirits have taken their flight, leaving friends to mourn and to sorrow over their tombs; and in that reverential feeling which leads the survivors not only to consecrate, but to adorn, the little spots of earth which contain all that is left of those whose living forms they once fondly cherished.

The custom which has long subsisted, and even at present subsists, in some parts of England, as well as of Wales, of planting evergreens around the graves, has been frequently touched upon, and has appeared to charm the fancy of the poet, as well as the heart of the man of sensibility. It is one indeed which is singularly pleasing, and is calculated to nourish the most delightful sensations of which perhaps human nature is susceptible. It seems as if we could not bear the remembrance of our friends to be associated with any thing but what is pure and lovely ; and, as if we fancied that while we can tend with tender care the shrubs that bloom around their ashes, we have still something which we can nourish for their sakes—something which, in imagination at any rate, can employ us in their service.

A few years ago, I was staying for some time at a little town upon the sea-coast, in the northern part of Wales. Upon the very skirts of the ocean rose a simple house of God, not in sculptured pride, or in massy grandeur, but humble and lowly as the religion to whose service it was dedicated ; and, while the Christian poured forth within its walls the sweet aspirations of piety, his prayers would mingle with the hoarse roaring of the waters, or the more distant murmur of the rippling waves, and forcibly reminding him of the dread power of Omnipotence, as well as that mercy which restrained its further exercise, would prompt him to utter still warmer effusions of reverence and of gratitude.

The ground on every side of this lowly edifice was devoted to the reception of the last sad remains of mortality; and its still inhabitants lay quietly side by side under the grassy mounds which covered them, and which were, some bound with the twisted osier,—some arrayed with a bright garment of flowers, strewed by the hand of affection. In one secluded corner, however, a green and fertile cluster caught the eye, and discovered a little enclosure, in which were planted shrubs and aromatic herbs, at whose roots a few purple violets hid their modest heads, and with the blushing rose and the scented myrtle, filled the air with their delicious perfume ; while a drooping willow at one end hung down its weeping branches over a marble tomb, and a grave cypress threw a darker shadow over the other. On one side of the tomb the following simple lines arrested the attention of the spectator:

Once lovely, pure, and good, on earth she dwelt,
T' infuse the heav'nly peace she inly felt;
To raise the drooping soul, to charm the heart,
And virtuous joy to all she lov'd, impart ;
While peaceful and serene, her spotless mind
No earthly passion tainted or confin'd.
But ah ! too pure in this mix'd scene to stay,
Her spirit sought to find a brighter way ;
A God of mercy view'd the struggling soul
Striving to free itself from earth's control,

Then in compassion stay'd th' unequal strife,
And burst the bonds that fasten'd it to life ;
Bid th' enraptur'd spirit soar on high,
And bloom for ever in its native sky.

On the opposite side were inscribed these words :

Here are deposited,
The remains of ELLEN,
Only surviving Daughter of MAJOR HOWELL ;
Who, at the early age of nineteen,
Was snatched by Death,
From her fond Parents,
And admiring Friends,
On the 5th day of August, 18——.

" The righteous shall see my face."

There was, near this sacred spot, a path leading
to a little eminence about an hundred yards distant
from the chapel, which I generally ascended twice
or thrice every day to inhale the pure sea breezes,
and to gaze on the blue expanse before me.   Here
could I stand or sit for hours, with my eyes fixed
upon this beautiful object, and my soul raised and
expanded by the nature of the emotions which it
excited.   I then experienced the justness of Addison's observation, that the imagination " loves to be
filled with an object, or to grasp at any thing that
is too big for its capacity ;" for mine certainly experienced the greatest delight in the contemplation
of a scene of which grandeur and immensity formed
the most striking features.

One soft sunny evening, when the waters lay
slumbering, as it were, in their capacious bed, and
reflecting as in a mirror the bright beams of the
setting sun ; and when that glorious orb was sinking gradually but majestically into the horizon, I
prepared to ascend to my usual station, that I
might catch its last parting rays, and behold them
apparently quenched in the ocean.   Before I had
reached the chapel, I perceived before me a female
figure, clothed, as I thought, in the " habiliments
of woe," and proceeding in the direction of the
little cemetery I have described ; but when, on
turning her head, she descried me in the distance,
she checked her steps, and walked slowly forward
in the path I was myself pursuing.   It immediately occurred to me, that this was some relative of
her whose bones were consigned to this last home,
and I resolved to be no impediment to the performance of the sacred offices which she was no
doubt come to fulfil.   I therefore quickened my
pace, and soon overtook the poor mourner, whose
face however was concealed by a long black veil,
but whose figure was commanding, and whose step
was dignified though solemn.   On quitting the
burial-ground, instead of proceeding up the hill, I
turned a little to the left, and placed myself behind
a jutting point of rock, from whence I could watch
her motions, without being myself visible.   In a

few seconds, I beheld her again approach the little cemetery, unlock the gate which led to it, and throw herself at the foot of the tomb, with her hands stretched upon the top, and her head resting upon them. When she had indulged her feelings for a few moments, she again arose, and stood with folded arms, gazing at this melancholy object, while her motionless form and sable garb seemed to fit her for the presiding Genius of so sad and yet so lovely a spot. Rousing from her meditation, she then employed herself in pulling a few withered leaves off the overshadowing willow, and in adjusting two or three plants in a form perhaps more tasteful and elegant. For some time she seemed to be thus occupied, when again she prostrated herself before the grave, clasped her hands fervently together, and raising her eyes towards heaven, appeared to be absorbed in mental devotion. Calmly she then arose, and, dropping her veil, seemed about to depart; but some tie, of more than mortal strength, drew her again to the inanimate marble. She paused—again turned away—and again looked back irresolute. 'Twas the last triumph she allowed to feeling. Waving her hand, as if bidding adieu to all most dear to her, she left the cemetery, fastened the entrance, and then, taking one long last look, departed; and I watched with interest her slowly-retreating figure, and her white hand-

kerchief, which she long held to her face, and
which convinced me, that she was indulging her
sorrow. " Poor mourner !" thought I, " thou hast
perhaps felt that pang more acute than every
other—the pang of being separated from the being
most precious to thy heart. May be from the tender plant, which, with maternal solicitude, thou
hast nourished and supported on thy bosom, and
hast watched over with anxious tenderness, and art
now left, like a tree stricken by the tempest, leaf-
less, bereaved, and desolate."

For three successive nights, I attended at the
same spot, and witnessed a nearly similar scene.
On each, did the same female appear, but on the
third, when I approached the little cemetery after
she had left it, I found that, the weather having
been dry and hot, she had refreshed the plants and
shrubs with water, and they sent forth a grateful
fragrance which perfumed the surrounding atmosphere.

I endeavoured to learn the story of the ill-fated
Ellen, and the interesting mourner whom I had
beheld sorrowing over her ashes; and I found that
they were indeed the pangs of a mother's heart,
which had caused the grief that I had witnessed.
She had attended her husband abroad through
many a scene of trial and of hardship;—she had
dressed his wounds upon the day of battle, and

she had watched over his soldier's lowly pallet with firm and unremitting tenderness; but his wounds were healed, and he rose from his sick-bed astonished at her magnanimity, and grateful for her affection. They returned together to their native country, that they might seek a reward for their past sufferings in the bosom of the land that gave them birth, and in the happy retirement which they best loved. Several children blessed their union; but some were nipped in the bud of infancy, and the rest prematurely destroyed, ere yet they were fully unfolded into blossoms. One beloved daughter——their beauteous Ellen——alone remained to them. All the tender shoots were withered, save this one, and her they cherished as their sole-remaining pride, their only surviving prop. They did not, however, allow their affections to blind their judgment, but subdued the strength of their attachment, that it might not be injurious to the character of their child. *That* child grew up all that her doating parents wished; and, lovely in mind as in person, she constituted their sum of happiness upon earth. But, alas! the sweetest and most delicate flowers are often nipped the soonest by the chill wind, or by the blighting mildew. Her fragile form but too easily sunk under the pressure of disease, and like a tender reed bent beneath its own unsupported weight. Her eyes

I

indeed sparkled with unusual lustre, but it was no more like the brilliance of health, than the false glare of a wandering meteor resembles the clear and steady effulgence of the meridian sun; and though a bright bloom coloured her cheek, it was not the rosy tint of vigour, but the harbinger of approaching ruin. The terrified parents beheld with horror the dreadful symptoms. In an agony of mind which none besides can fully appreciate, they tried all that nature dictated, or art devised, to stop the progress of the fatal malady. But it was too late. It made rapid and gigantic strides, and hope itself was soon compelled to droop in anguish. The lovely victim saw her fate before her, but her wings were plumed for heaven, and she wished not to hover longer upon the earth. While her body drooped and languished, her mind became strengthened and purified, and the undecaying spirit seemed to shine forth more visibly and more beautifully, when the mortal shroud which enveloped it was gradually falling away. But though she grieved not for herself, she yet mourned for those whom she felt that her death would make but too desolate, and she tried to reconcile them to the prospect of her loss, and to prepare them to bear it with fortitude. This task she essayed unceasingly to complete, and she thought her labour was rewarded, for her nearly heart-

broken parents affected before her a calmness
which they could not feel, because they saw that
it gave her pleasure. At length, life gradually
waned,—and waned,—until its lamp shot up one
bright but quivering gleam, and was then darkened
for ever ! She was dead—but the rose still lived in
her cheek, and a smile still played upon the half-
closed lips whose last accents had breathed the
fond name of Mother ! and those who looked upon
her could scarcely believe but that she still sweetly
slept. But there were *two* hearts which felt how
surely she had left them for ever. Awake to an
agonizing sense of the reality of their misfortune,
the unhappy parents gave way for some time to
the bitterness of their feelings. They saw around
them a dreary waste, without one pleasant spot on
which their eyes could rest with joy. The houris
of their paradise had disappeared, and with her its
enchantment vanished. The poor bereaved mother first forgot the creature in the Christian.
Leaning upon the " Rock of Ages," she rose above
her grief, and bid her anguish cease, and her sighs
be hushed. Her heart still indeed bled, but she
stanched the wound by the efforts of piety. Her
tears would still flow, but she dried them with religious hope ; and if a murmur dared to hover on
her lips, she dismissed it with religious horror.

Man, although perhaps better able to bear without intoxication the inebriating scenes of prosperity, is often, when at last he has been depressed by misfortune, less able to rise from beneath its pressure; as the tough oak, when once bent, cannot be again uplifted like the youthful ash, or the slender willow. Thus it was with her stricken husband. No gleam of comfort seemed to enlighten the dark gloom which enshrouded his heart,—no ray of consolation penetrated there;—for, absorbed in one overwhelming consciousness, he sought not to alleviate, or to diminish his sorrow. But, animated by trusting faith, his virtuous wife essayed to open to him a more cheering prospect; and, concealing the misery of her own, she tried to awaken in his soul, some brighter feelings. Approving Heaven beheld, and smiled upon her endeavours,—the dawn of revived happiness gradually opened upon his mind,—the sun of religious hope illumined his path,—and though he did not cease to mourn, he yet mourned not as " one that had no hope."

Afraid to trust his beholding often the spot which contained the ashes of his child, this noble-minded female attended every evening to perform alone, and unassisted, save by the unseen arm which is " mighty " to support, as well as " to save," the sacred offices of affection; to ease her full heart at the tomb of her lamented daughter, and to implore divine aid and a fresh accession of heavenly grace; and then——to return with a serene and placid countenance, to bless and support the partner in her affliction.

Such is the glorious spirit which is infused into the breast by the blessed light, and by the consolatory truths, of religion. Such is the strength which may be derived from the sure anchor of faith. No other principle but this could sustain the soul through the severe trials of mortality, or give it firmness and stability to bear the angry storm, or the beating tempest. None but this can guide the wanderer safely through the wilderness of life, or bestow upon him, at its termination, the glorious meed of immortality.

BENEVOLENCE.

True benevolence should constantly influence both our feelings and our manners, and be displayed in trifles as well as in greater things.

To some amiable and well-regulated minds, there is scarcely any thing which affords a sweeter or more continual gratification than the interchange of those various kindnesses and attentions with our fellow-creatures, which are suggested by warm and delicate feelings, and are the genuine offspring of piety and benevolence. To the man of the world, the unthinking, the heartless, or the selfish, they appear perhaps useless, foolish, or trivial; but to a soul whereon are stamped the kindly and sympathetic affections of nature, they afford constant scope for the indulgence of all those soft and endearing sensibilities which are the source of so much good and so much pleasure.

It is not the laboured panegyric, the glittering or valuable gift, or the high-flown compliment, that can touch the heart, or wake the throb of earnest gratitude. No; they may fan the flame of vanity, or seduce, for a moment, by their own deceitful brilliancy;

but it is for the look of love, the glance of sympathy, the voice of pitying consolation, and the thousand acts of tender and friendly interest, by which we can mitigate the sorrows, or add to the happiness of others,—to win for us their love, and to awaken for us their cordial esteem.

When the soul is bowed down by the consciousness of weakness, or perhaps of guilt, and shrinks from the gaze of its fellow mortals, as from the severity of eager and unpitying criticism, how may one soft word, one encouraging look, open it to the tide of repressed affection, and stifled repentance! How may the discriminating kindness of a friend lead gradually from folly or from wickedness, to peace, to virtue, and to God!

Again, when oppressed by undeserved neglect, harassed by poverty, or stung by the rude tauntings of upstart ignorance, the heart, galled by recent and unprovoked ill-treatment, renounces all commerce with the beings of this world, and spurns them from it with the irascibility of injured innocence,—how delightful to pour gradually upon it the balm of humanity and tenderness! How gratifying to pay all those quiet, delicate, and respectful attentions, which can neither alarm the watchful vigilance of pride, nor rouse the humbled, but not exterminated spirit! How sweet to watch the gradual dawnings of that refreshing light which the Almighty has given us to cheer our pilgrimage, but which had been darkened by forgetfulness or inhumanity, and to see cheerfulness, forgiveness, and brotherly love, again diffusing their soft beams over the before desolated soul.

Such a blessed work as this, however, may perhaps be said to show the *perfection* of that spirit which I so highly applaud, and indisputable as are its claims to merit, few I should imagine could do otherwise than acknowledge them ; but then, whilst admiring the effect, they will still, perhaps, disregard the subsidiary means by which it was produced, and these, therefore, I think are not sufficiently valued or attended to. People are too apt to consider as below their notice, those numberless acts of forbearance, consideration, or kindness, for performing which opportunities occur at every turn in the road of life, but which, like the flowers of the field, have their humble beauties and modest fragrance passed by unnoticed. Many there are, possessing warm hearts, and excellent dispositions, who are yet not alive to the delight of dispensing to others those little favours which daily and hourly present themselves ; or, who undervalue them because they are of no great consequence in themselves ; but let them remember what that admirable female writer whom I have before quoted tells us, that

"Trifles make up the sum of human things."

And consider, that if these *apparent* trifles possess the power of giving pleasure to others, they at once raise themselves to great comparative importance.

It was just upon feelings and principles such as these, that an excellent female relative of mine used constantly to act, and from seeing them exemplified in her in their most beautiful form, I doubt not I first imbibed that extreme love and veneration for them which I remember to have always entertained. She was indeed a pattern of moderation, of forbearance, and of Christian charity; the milk of human kindness warmed her heart, the pulse of tender sympathy beat in her bosom, and, though severe in her judgment of herself, she was ever candid and compassionate in her estimate of others. Every one who surrounded, or were in any way within the sphere of her influence, basked in the sunshine of her benevolence. Active duties were by her assiduously performed; but besides these, she eminently excelled in displaying those passive kindnesses which, although silent and unobtrusive, yet find their way to the hearts of those towards whom they are displayed. No one could approach her without being unconsciously charmed by that

certain something in her manner which spoke a
wish either to gratify or to spare the feelings of
others; and many, unable to define what it was
that possessed such an irresistible attraction, yet
willingly owned that such an attraction *did* subsist,
and that in her society they felt a pleasure for
which they were unable entirely to account. Alas!
she is gone to that bourn, from whence "no traveller returns;" but I see her now, pictured on my
memory as she once was in the days of my youth,
with her nicely plaited cap, her white handkerchief
arranged in neat folds across her bosom, and the
high-heeled shoes which gave her such dignity in
my boyish imagination,—and again dwell upon her
mild but expressive eyes, which seemed at once to
awe and repress vice, while they courted and encouraged humble virtue,—the sweet light of the
soul which diffused its heavenly glow upon the
countenance, and the flash of sudden animation
which would illumine it, when the sight or the recital of some deed of goodness called forth her admiring approbation. But that the greatness as
well as the beauty of her mind may be estimated
by the reader, I will briefly unfold one part of her
life which will, I think, effectually display it. In
her youth she was extremely enthusiastic, susceptible of the warmest affections, and incredulous of
any thing like treachery or deceit. She had a

friend nearly of her own age, whom she loved with almost idolizing tenderness. For years their hearts were open to each other, the thoughts of each unhesitatingly disclosed, its feelings fearlessly expressed. This friend was one of Nature's most beautiful productions: her bright dark eyes beamed mingled rays of sweetness and intelligence; her polished forehead was shaded by her locks of brilliant jet. The unspotted whiteness of her complexion contrasted with the sweet bloom that tinged her cheeks; while her figure, of the finest proportions and most perfect symmetry, arrested the eye by the natural grace of its movements, and the unstudied elegance of its attitudes. She, to whom envy and jealousy were unknown,—the pure, the unsophisticated Helen, delighted in gazing upon the charms of her friend, and in pointing them out to the admiration of others; while that friend herself appreciated Helen's mental perfections, and appeared to return her affection with almost equal ardour; but her character was less stable, and her principles less firm. Their mutual love " grew with their growth, and strengthened with their strength," and year after year passed on, gilded by the pleasures of friendship, and the buoyant hopes of youth. Together they traced the sacred truths of inspiration, together wandered through the gay and diversified map of nature, and together gazed with transport upon its sublime or beautiful features. They had long no wish beyond the gratification of pursuits the most innocent, and feelings the most amiable and praiseworthy. But, in an evil hour, the lovely Sophia received a pressing invitation from an aunt who resided in the metropolis, in the midst of gaiety which she loved, and the votary of Fashion, which she worshipped. The hour of separation came: it was the first they had ever experienced, and the two friends as yet little acquainted with sorrow, wept upon each other's bosom with intense and bitter anguish. Again, and again, they parted, and returned to take a last embrace; till, by one strong effort, they tore themselves asunder, never, alas! to be again united in the bonds of such unsullied purity.

A short time after her friend's departure, a cousin of the amiable Helen returned from India, where he had been for many years. He was handsome, lively, and well-informed, with a disposition like her own, ardent and enthusiastic, unrestrained, however, like her's, by strong and unswerving principle. A reciprocity of taste and sentiments drew them towards each other, aided by the delight with which the inquiring Helen listened to his observations upon foreign scenes and manners, and the gratification he naturally felt in being an object of attention to a young female, adorned by many

personal as well as mental charms; for although
not possessed of the dazzling beauty of Sophia,
she was in a high degree both interesting and
attractive. In fine, his heart soon yielded to
charms which every day dawned upon him afresh,
and he told his tale of love to an ear too ready to
listen to its bewitching accents. They who have
tasted the inspiring emotions of a first love, may
imagine those of the susceptible Helen. It existed
in her spotless bosom with all the freshness of novelty, and the purity of perfect innocence. It was
enshrined in her soul, as a thing that was holy and
sacred, and cherished as a gem of inestimable value,
upon which her future happiness must entirely depend. So highly blessed in love and friendship,
she almost wondered at her own happy fate. The
present was passed in joy,—the future seemed
arrayed in bright and glowing colours, and every
scene on which her eyes rested, tinged by the magic
influence of love, appeared marked with new and
matchless beauties.

But too soon was the spell broken, too quickly
the bright vision of fancy faded and dispersed;
for, alas! not on earth is innocence proof against
misfortune, or shielded from the attacks of guilt.
Like its own emblem, the dove, it can find no place
on which to rest with security in this world, but it

has a protector to whom it still can fly—a heavenly ark to which it can turn for refuge.

Helen's happy lover was called to town, and she sent by him an epistle to her friend, acquainting her with her happiness, drawing with the pencil of love the character of her future husband, and assuring her that only one thing was necessary to her perfect felicity,—her beloved Sophia's approbation of the choice of her heart.   The answer to this appeared to her cold, and unlike what she expected from her friend, but it contained high encomiums of her " handsome lover," and she tried to be satisfied, and to convince herself that she was either fanciful or unreasonable.   Time passed, and she heard less frequently from her beloved, less affectionately from her friend.   She became uneasy, she knew not why ; anxious, she could not tell for what ; but still not even a transient suspicion ever crossed her mind to the prejudice of those most dear to her.   The dreadful truth, therefore, broke upon her when utterly unprepared for its appalling nature.   In one bitter moment, she learnt that her lover was base, her friend faithless ; that she had to bewail her own desertion, and to weep for their complicated guilt.   The horror of their perfidy, the keen sense of deprivation, the wretched consciousness of disappointed affection, and wound-

ed dignity,—all these, and many other bitter feelings which necessarily agitated her breast, may be
more easily conceived than described. Life, which
had so lately appeared to her gay and blooming,
now seemed as a dreary waste,—cold, barren, and
cheerless. All that had brightened it was gone,
and she had nothing left but sorrow and despair.
A fever, the consequence of contending and violent
emotions, seized her brain; and it was long thought
that the blow which had deprived her of happiness
would bereave her of reason. But no! that precious gift was still left her by a merciful Providence, to be afterwards her guide to peace, and a
shining light to herself and others. She rose in a
few months from her bed of suffering, powerless in
her body, and depressed in mind, but with a calm
expression of resignation settled in her countenance,
and a look of mild and patient endurance which
woke the throb of mingled piety and admiration in
the hearts of all who beheld her. She never spoke
of her sorrow, she never adverted even to her misfortune; but as soon as she was able, she resolutely
engaged herself in active pursuits, and sedulously
strove to find constant employment for her thoughts.
It was a beautiful sight to see one so young struggling with, and finally mastering, her sorrow; to
behold her disciplining her mind, as it were, to suffering, subduing even her passions and her feelings,

and soaring almost above the weaknesses of humanity. Doubtless, she rested not only upon her own unsupported strength, but with pious humility sought for that divine aid which can support the soul through the dark regions of misery, and lead it gradually into the cheering light of hope and comfort. And she *did* regain composure, she was even sometimes sensible of joy; but it was not a joy like what she had once felt——rapid, violent, and irrepressible,——but mild, quiet, and temperate; such as those feel who have been injured by the storms, or who have learned justly to appreciate the transitory pleasures of life. She had long forgiven those who had so deeply wounded her; she even pined to hear that they were happy, and to tell them she wished their happiness, but she dared not trust herself to inquire about them; or rather, she dreaded to have her secret hopes destroyed. Thus years passed on, and she knew nothing of them but that they existed; when one day, she heard by the merest accident, that she whom she had once loved as the friend of her bosom, had deserted her husband and her home, and was in her turn forsaken, and concealed no one knew where. On learning this dreadful intelligence, the senses of poor Helen forsook her; but they did not desert her long. She had too important a task to perform, to attend to her own sufferings; she was resolved to discover the abode of the guilty Sophia, and if possible to lead her back to the path of rectitude. "Alas! alas!" she exclaimed with bitterness, "she may be ill, or perhaps dying, without a friend to cheer her last moments, or in whose bosom she can repose her griefs, or ease her upbraiding conscience. But thou shalt not be long deserted or forlorn; I will still be to thee a friend, and Oh! may I, by the blessing of God, restore thee to virtue."

Her fears were realized. After making many fruitless inquiries, she at length discovered the once beautiful Sophia—stretched on the couch of sickness, and surrounded by penury and wretchedness; but like an angel of mercy she hovered round her miserable form, procured for her every necessary comfort, and attended upon her night and day with unwearied and unremitting care. At length, her efforts were rewarded,—her unhappy patient revived to a sense of her own wretchedness, and her friend's generosity. A sullen shame at first took possession of her breast, but the gentle Helen, by her pitying accents, and tender attentions, broke through its cold frost-work, and let in the stream of stifled affection. Then did she become the physician of her soul. Then did she gradually lead the poor sinner to the purifying fount of repentance, and when the sense of her

K

guilt was ready to overwhelm her with despair, did she point out the path which was still left to lead her back into the " perfect way," and open her mind to the blessed influence of religious hope. But this was no easy task—she had to endure the fretful complainings of weakness, the tormenting fears of guilt, and the vacillating resolves of newly-awakened piety ; but, strong in faith, and firm in purpose, she accomplished the blessed work ; and then, when the world would have scoffed at, and even the virtuous would have shunned the victim of licentious passion, she took her to her quiet home, and by every means which the most humane benevolence could suggest, sought to divert her mind from the painful subject which usually occupied it.

" Oh! Helen !" said the poor young creature one day as she sat with her hand clasped in that of her friend, and her eyes glistening with the tear of gratitude—" Oh, Helen ! what a mind, what a heart is yours ! I, who have sinned so greatly,—who have injured you so severely, even I, when my own guilt has plunged me into wretchedness, you take again to your bosom without one word of reproach, one upbraiding look. Oh Helen ! Helen ! that I had but before known how to value you." Here, overwhelmed with her feelings of contrition, she clasped her hands before her eyes, and burst into a flood of tears ; but the soft voice of pity which had often before calmed her painful emotions, soon, like oil upon the troubled waters, soothed her repentant spirit; and, with deep humiliation, she proceeded to relate her gradual progress in the path of sin, from the moment that she had been introduced into the gay scenes of the metropolis. Intoxicated by the flattery which immediately overwhelmed her, she said, all else besides the gratification of her vanity soon became distasteful to her, and, immersed in constant dissipation, she had no time to discover the dangerous state of her own mind. "Such was my situation," continued she, "when my—my—your lover arrived, Helen. He was, you know, strikingly handsome, and you also perhaps are aware, an enthusiastic admirer of beauty. Alas! I too soon discovered it, and, vain of my personal attractions, I played off every fascination to captivate his senses. At first, my sole purpose was to gratify my own overweening love of conquest, without an idea of any serious termination to what I had learnt to consider as so common-place a thing; but there was something in my new admirer (for such he soon became) so superior to the set of cold-hearted fashionists with whom I usually associated, that, before I was aware of it, I found that the dart which I meant should only slightly graze his bosom, had deeply wounded my own. Spare me—

you know the rest. Helen! *dear* Helen, can you ever forgive me?" " Yes, Sophia; yes, my love," replied the agitated Helen, endeavouring to resume her firmness, " I *do* forgive you, but Oh! Sophia, how ought the first approaches of sin to be watched and overcome! How ought the whispers of inclination to be examined and controlled!" " They ought, they ought indeed, Helen. Would that I had once checked mine, and I should not be what I am now. I should not have suffered the agonies I have for years endured,—for never! Oh never have I known peace since I took that first fatal step. Never could I forget, amidst all the triumphs of my vanity, that I had deceived my friend, but instead of sueing for and endeavouring to deserve her forgiveness, I tried to stifle the upbraidings of conscience by plunging deeper in dissipation. Even my husband I disgusted, and then, in desperation, giving the rein to my passions, I——" She could not complete the appalling confession; and her compassionate hearer, grieved at her distress, and almost overcome by her own, only silently grasped the cold hand which was locked in hers, and then quitted the room.

Dire indeed was the throb of agony with which she sometimes gazed on the wan face and faded form of her once charming Sophia, and thought of the time when she had loved to look on them, and to think the soul to which they were united was as pure and perfect as themselves. Often did she recall her buoyant step, her animated glances, her tone of happy gaiety, and then look at the sunken eye, the melancholy countenance, and the attenuated figure before her, (which spoke silently but forcibly the approaching strides of death,) and wish that it might please the Almighty to take them together to himself; for, fallen as she was, she still loved her, but with a love so holy, that it contained little of the dross of earth, much of the purity of heaven, and to that heaven she longed to accompany the expectant soul, and see it accepted at the mercy-seat of the Most High. But this was not to be, and she prepared to endure the trial which awaited her, with the patience and the fortitude of a Christian. Every day the poor sufferer became more weaned from earthly things, and more abounding in trusting faith. She saw that her end was approaching, and she perceived it with joy, for she hoped that she was forgiven by her Maker, and she had little left her upon earth.

" Helen," said she, one evening as her friend was sitting by the side of her bed, to which she had been some time confined. " Helen ! thou art indeed ' *faithful unto death*,' but though *that* may divide us, say—shall we—shall we not meet again?"

" I trust, I fervently trust so, my love," replied

Helen, sinking on her knees, and raising her eyes, as if to supplicate it might be so. "In that heaven where death can never enter, I trust we shall dwell together to all eternity." "Oh! 'tis a transporting thought, Helen! and unlimitable is that divine mercy which can allow it to such a wretch as I—" she paused awhile, and then solemnly continued—"I feel something within me that tells me I am pardoned by my God, and in that blessed hope I shall draw my last breath in peace. But—I had one wish—I dared not to express it, Helen—but it would have cheered my soul to have heard my husband say, 'I forgive you.'" At this moment, Helen's attentive ear caught the sound of a carriage—she scarcely breathed—it stopped. She then took the feeble hand of her friend. "And should you like to see him, Sophia?" "What do you mean, Helen? Oh trifle not with me. Tell me—Is he come?"

"Be calm, dearest: I have indeed sent for him, for I knew it would rejoice him to see you." "Oh! I see—I feel all—he is here. Bring him to me, that I may hear his forgiveness. For I feel——" A deadly paleness overspread her countenance, and a convulsive shivering seized her form. The terrified Helen raised and supported her upon her bosom. In the same moment the door opened. The dying Sophia beheld her husband enter, and with a strong effort she half sprung as if to meet him. But nature was exhausted; she fell back into the arms of her faithful friend,—faintly murmured, " Forgive me,"—raised her eyes in one fixed upward gaze,—and her spirit fled for ever.

Her friend was gone from her; and Helen was almost alone in the mansion of her fathers, for her parents had long been dead, and she had no one near her, save an elderly female, who was distantly related to, and usually resided with her. But the good can never be in want of friends. By a long course of uninterrupted benevolence, she acquired more than any one I ever knew; and, like a star of brightness, she irradiated the path which Providence had destined for her upon earth; and when her course was run, its setting beams were cheered by the holy light of religion, and soothed by the remembrance of deeds of virtue and of charity.

HOME.

———

HOME ! the very word itself looks smiling and joyous, and its fair honest aspect, unlike too many other things in this pretending world, excites emotions of pleasure which it can afterwards realize and cherish. What a crowd of pleasurable sensations does it raise in the breast ! What a thrill of happiness does it cause ! Like the sound of pure and perfect harmony, it can, in the pure and unsophisticated heart, still every unruly passion, hush every angry and unquiet feeling, and shed a calm and placid serenity upon the heart. And if the name can often do all this, what can the reality perform ! What happiness can home itself, with all its comforts, all its consoling joys, animate and diffuse ! Ah ! but those only, who have in some sort suffered sorrow and disappointment from without ; they who have been buffeted about by the conflicting tumults of the world ; they who have discovered that what the world terms pleasure is in itself but mockery, and that pomp and show

are generally but the gaudy coverings of misery,—
they who are sickened by the crouching servility
of hypocrites, or the unmeaning professions of
fashion,—or they who *have* been alone amidst a
crowd of human beings, in which there was not
one who could enter into their joys or their sorrows, or to whom they were bound by any tie of
love or sympathy,—they, and they *only* can know
how to value, in its fullest sense, the serenity, the
peacefulness, the tenderness, the independence,
and the sincerity of home. They, and they only,
can truly experience the awakening bliss which its
recollections or its prospect can in an instant communicate. It is the little spot upon this wide
earth to which the eyes of the wanderer are directed, even while he is exploring unknown regions and traversing new lands. It is the soothing
opiate which lulls the weary soldier, when his ears
have been stunned with the din of battle, and his
sight has been assailed by scenes of horror. It is
the magnet which impels the adventurous youth
through the perils of the ocean, and makes him
brave with unwearied courage the stern and conflicting elements,—the haven in which he is to
repose after the tempest, and where he is to seek
peace from the whirlwind.

And even to those who have placed their hopes
upon the phantom Fame, and who are climbing up

the steep and intricate paths of ambition,—those who are courted and caressed, and on whose heads, honours are lavishly showered, Home sometimes proves a refuge from anxiety, and a grateful retirement from the unsatisfying enjoyments of grandeur; and when the dream of vanity has fled, —and when the vapours of flattery are dispersed, with what a feeling of thankfulness will they then turn to this hitherto rejected blessing,—this bourn of peace, which they forsook in their prosperity, but which will open to them its fostering arms when deserted and sorrowful. Yes, for it is only to the decidedly vicious,—to those whose hearts are debased by sin, and whose taste has been vitiated by a long course of unlawful pleasures, that *Home* denies its pure and healing influence. To them indeed its joys must ever be flat and distasteful, and to the weak and the frivolous they may perhaps offer but a transient allurement; but from both these classes may the bulk of my countrymen be ever excluded,—may they still take an honest pride in the comforts of their " ain fire sides,"— may they glory in the sacred privacy of their dwellings,—and confine their warmest desires within their hallowed limits. May *Home* long be the talisman that nerves the hand, the music that charms the ear, and the reward that best crowns the toils and the labours of an *Englishman*.

I had, some years ago, a high gratification in witnessing the return, to the bosom of a peaceful and valuable home, of an only son, whose amiable character had justly endeared him to his family. I was passing through the town of ———, where lived one who had been in my youth the friend to whose superior wisdom I had looked up for advice in many a critical emergency, as additional years had granted him additional experience, but had diminished nothing of the openness, the mildness, or the winning suavity which are so alluring in the gay and buoyant spring-time of existence. He was now declining slowly into its autumnal vale, and he was laden with the golden fruits of that fertile season, without having caught its most sombre and melancholy tinges. He was still to me the friend that he ever had been; and, with that delightful feeling at my heart, which almost all must experience at the prospect of again seeing those they best love, I hastened to spend one night at least beneath his hospitable roof. When I claimed admittance at his door, however, the impatience which burned in my veins was somewhat cooled by the tardiness with which my summons was answered, although, from the sounds which reached my ear from within, I felt assured that there were many persons who might have allowed me ingress. Again I applied myself to the knocker, and a

servant appeared with hurry in her manner, and
her cheeks glowing with that sort of colour which
is given by any unusual excitement, and ushered
me in with an air of uncertainty which told me
that she was dubious whether my visit would be
acceptable.

I had not seen my friend for some years, and I
expected to find some of the marks which time
leaves in its progress over the face of man.   But
I had no leisure to search for them.   I found him
pacing with a quick step up and down a spacious
apartment, with an open letter in his hand, on
which his tears freely rolled.   At first, I feared
that I was come to the house of mourning; but
one glance at his countenance sufficed to remove
this apprehension, for on it was legibly written the
ripe fulness of joy, which was indeed clothed in
the emblems, though it partook in nothing of the
nature of grief.   But, alas! so closely are happiness and sorrow connected together in this imperfect scene, that the link which serves to perfect the
bright chain of the one, is closely allied to that
which commences the gloomy bonds of the other;
and even while we think ourselves encircled by the
first, we feel the approaching pressure of the latter.
When he beheld me, he wiped away the drops that
were trembling in his eyes, and eagerly advanced
to meet me.   " Welcome, thrice welcome, my

dearest friend, you are come in a happy hour.
This letter—my boy—." " Is he returned ? Is
he safe ?" I eagerly interrupted. " Safe—safe—
returned, and will be with us in half an hour.
Congratulate me," he continued, as he fervently
pressed my hand, " I thought I might never see
my boy again, and Heaven has brought him back
to bless his fond father's sight before the hand of
death tears him away for ever." The full, uplifted eye,—the sunny smile of gratitude,—told me
what was passing in his thoughts. ·He was one
whose sight was never fixed upon the blessing,
without contemplating the source from which it
flowed. His soul was then with his God,—prostrate in thankful adoration !

When the first burst of his feelings was over, he
read to me the letter which announced the joyful
intelligence of the return of the young sailor, after
a tedious absence on a long and dangerous expedition; adding, that I must not expect at present
to see the delighted mother and sisters, " who,"
said he, smiling, " are making as many prepara-
tions for the arrival of the youngster, as if he were
not one of our own ' kith and kin ;' but when the
mind is joyous, the body is disposed to activity,
and to sit down expecting him, and counting the
tedious moments till his arrival, would be impossible. By the by," added he, starting from his

chair, as if to prove the truth of this declaration, " there is one order that I must give, pardon me a moment—" and away he hurried, more, I felt assured, for the sake of finding occupation, than because he had real business to transact. The sounds of bustle meantime increased, and I could not but smile to think of all the little comforts that were probably preparing for this youthful son of Neptune, who had been so long surrounded by danger, and in the daily endurance of innumerable hardships. " Now," thought I, " will he taste, in their greatest perfection, the sweets of *Home*, for they will strike upon his heart and senses with double force, when for some time they have been withheld. What an ungrateful thing is human nature, that nothing but a temporary deprivation of the blessings which surround it, can make them be duly felt—nothing but suffering pierce through the mist of morose discontent that envelops it, and open upon it the cheering light which is always ready to shed around its delightful influence." While I was musing on reflections such as these, and looking forward with pleasure to the contemplation of the scene I had so opportunely arrived to witness, the happy mother entered the room, followed by the smiling Ellen, and the more pensive Emilia, the one, with her laughing cheeks flushed with expectation, the other with

a look of placid enjoyment diffused over her
features. By all I was cordially welcomed, and,
as my friend entered almost at the same moment,
we formed ourselves into a social circle round the
cheerful hearth, though not to talk, for scarcely a
word was uttered, but every now an then an expanding smile on one of the surrounding countenances told the thoughts which were operating
within, while the restless perturbed movements of
the rest spoke an anxious impatience which could
scarcely be controlled. Occasionally, also, one or
other remembered that " such a thing" was not
done,—that " something else" had been forgotten,
—that " dear Edward" always used to be fond of
" so and so,"—and that such an arrangement
should be made to surprise him. At length, however, all this was brought to an end by the magic
of sound alone. The distant roll of a carriage
struck upon every ear, and for an instant was listened to in breathless silence. In the next, all
started from their seats, and " It is—it is my boy:
It is—it is Edward," was ejaculated by all. The
mother and sisters hastened to the door, though it
must be some minutes before the carriage could
reach it. The father stood up, and clasped his
hands together, then drew a long deep breath, as
if he felt that choking sensation which violent emotion will produce, and seemed endeavouring to

repress an agitation which almost subdued him. The carriage rolled round the corner of the house, —the smoking horses were hastily pulled up, while the gravel rattled under their unsteady hoofs. The door was opened by an invisible hand, and the youthful sailor was in an instant within the expanded arms of his mother ! " My son ! my *best* boy !" murmured from her lips, and—" Edward, *dear* Edward, let me look at you," I heard uttered by the speaking accents of sisterly affection. 'Twas a moment of such pure and delicious happiness, as mortals are rarely allowed to taste, like a bright and golden drop, glittering amid surrounding gloom. " But my father, where is my father ?" exclaimed the grateful son, as he burst from the tender bonds which maternal love had encircled around him, and looking anxiously and eagerly on every side. " Here—here," replied the agitated parent, struggling for composure, as he sprang forwards, and clasped its dearest treasure with fervent pressure to his heart :—and there, in that sacred spot, I left him, like a promising, but still tender sapling, twining about the aged and majestic oak, and seeking protection in its bosom.

And can earth be the scene of misery that some will paint it ? Can it be the region of desolation and of woe, in which sorrow and despair alone abide, when it exhibits such scenes as these upon its surface? And is man only the child of sin and sorrow, when he is capable of feelings so rich and so ecstatic? No; he is fallen, he is debased; his beauty is tarnished, his splendour is defiled, but it is not *extinguished*, and he can yet emit sparks of his original brightness, to speak the inhabitant of Paradise, and the creature who had borne the impress of divinity; while that great Being whom he has offended, still surrounds him with innumerable blessings, and places many and various pleasures within his reach. Of these, few partake less of " earthly mould," those which spring from love and friendship; and seldom does humanity appear under a more alluring form than when it is under their softening influence.

When I rejoined the delighted group from whom I had lately flown, I found the young wanderer seated between his two sisters, who were each assailing him with a thousand questions in a breath, not one of which he could find even an instant to answer; while the fond parents were gazing on him with speechless love, dwelling on every dear and well-remembered feature, and noting with parental pride how each was ripened into manly and expressive beauty. " Dear Edward, how you are grown!" exclaimed the lively Ellen, measuring him with a quick glance of unconcealed admiration, " and I declare," putting her fingers gently under

L

one of his redundant locks, " the sea-winds have
not destroyed my dearly-beloved curls, but how
you *are* sun-burnt!"— " Sailors have little of
either time or inclination to heed their complexions,
Ellen," replied her brother, laughing.   " But
come, since you are criticising my beautiful person,
I wonder what you have been doing with yours,
since I can hardly recognise my little good-tem-
pered, romping play-fellow, in this tall blooming
sister by my side."   " Ah, brother, but you will
still, to your cost, find that she is the same identical foolish mad-cap, and she bears one thing about
her that she prizes dearly—see," pointing to the
girdle which confined her slender waist, " the present that you gave your little Ellen the day before
you left us; here it is, you see, to grace your return."   " You are a good dear girl," he replied,
glancing at her with delighted tenderness, and im-
printing a fraternal kiss upon her blushing cheek.
" And my gentle Amelia," turning to his other
sister, whose pleasing countenance was beaming
with even more than usual sweetness, " ever the
same,—and with, I dare say, that *same* love of the
romantic that I used to have the wickedness to
laugh at you for.   Well, I have heaps of adventures and ' hair-breadth escapes ' to charm your
fancy with, so prepare yourself to listen in wondering silence."   " And you are to be my hero, and a

man of war the enchanted castle, in which you
perform sundry deeds of valour; but where is the
fair lady who is to animate your exertions?" asked
she, with an arch smile. "Where, but by my
side, Amelia, strengthening my arm, and animating
my heart. Glory is the mistress of your brother's
breast!" and the very word itself, possessing almost
talismanic power, diffused a fine glow over his open
brow, and made his eyes sparkle with additional
lustre. At this moment, a man-servant who had
been many years in the family, and was warmly
attached to it, entered the room to "look once
more," as he said, "upon his dear young master's
face;" upon which the generous youth sprung up,
and hastened to meet him with extended hand,
while the old man, bowing low, seemed scarcely to
know whether or not he ought to accept it, till he
felt his own affectionately and cordially grasped,
and then his honest heart, mounting to his eyes,
suffused them with tears of grateful joy. "There
is another friend wants to see you, master Edward,"
said he, after the lapse of a few minutes, "Poor
Carlo had like to have died with grief after you
were gone, and I do think he knows you are come
back again, for he whined at the door till I let him
in, and he's been following me about since, and
looking up in my face for all the world as if he
was asking me to bring him to you." "Then I

am sure you shall grant his petition, Jonathan,
Carlo was my faithful companion for many a year,"
replied Edward, smiling at his ready explanation
of the animal's mute language; and the old man
immediately departed, but returned in an instant,
accompanied by the discerning Carlo, who, as if
in confirmation of his assertions, bounded into the
room, and with a cry of joy, jumped with wild
transport upon the well-remembered form before
him, and seemed to court some mark of his cogni-
zance and approbation. Nor did he sue in vain,
for after being loaded with caresses, he took his
station for the night at the feet of his former
master, and by his mute but expressive demonstra-
tions of pleasure, gave a finish to this picture of
domestic felicity.

And thus, in the interchange of mutual affection,
and the gratification of anxious and innocent curiosity, passed an evening on which I always look
back with a feeling of inward satisfaction, and on
which I have dwelt, perhaps, too long for the
patience of my readers. But let them remember,
that if I do enlarge upon what may be termed trifles, they are of that kind which assist in consti-
tuting the mighty sum of human happiness, and on
which the mind can rest with innocence, if not with
improvement. I confess that I have ever been a
minute and pleased observer of all the little private

dramas of life, the events of which I eagerly participate, listening with delight to the artless expressions of natural affection, and watching the
various modes in which character developes its
secret nature. While others are perhaps interesting themselves in the fate of empires, or scruti-
nizing the affairs of mighty nations, I turn to trace
the windings of the human heart, and feast upon
scenes of quiet joy, and unobtrusive happiness.

> *These* touch the chord that vibrates at my heart,
> As if with magic power; awakening there
> That full deep int'rest which arrests the soul,
> And soothes its varying passions.

A COUNTRY SUNDAY.

How calmly and sweetly breaks the Sabbath morn upon the soul of the Christian! What a pure and holy light seems to hover over and illuminate it! What a mild and beautiful radiance does it cast around! As a place of rest is greeted with delight by the weary traveller, or as a spring of water is viewed with eager eyes by the thirsty wanderer, who, in traversing the wild and sandy desert, where no trace of verdure is seen to cheer his prospect, and no brook appears to cool his parched tongue, or bathe his feverish limbs,—so does this day of peace beam upon the longing eye, and gladden and refresh the pious heart. It is the bourn to which it looks upon the earth, for refuge from bustle and from turmoil,—the support on which it leans during trouble or affliction,—the pleasant spot, to which it turns from the gloom or the anxieties of the world; and where, after having been for a time tost to and fro on the tumultuous ocean of life, it may repose awhile in safety, and gain fresh strength and renovated spirits.

In the lovely month of July, this day once opened with a glorious splendour. That bright luminary, the sun, rose sublimely from the horizon, and cast its brilliant rays upon every object. The green fields, and the variegated hedges were be-spangled with dew, which glittered in its beams, and the limpid stream reflected it in its bosom, as it murmured gently along. I ascended a rising eminence, to contemplate a scene so sweet and gra-tifying; and, inspired with the delightful sensations to which it gave birth, I allowed them utterance in the following unstudied lines :—

Oh hail! thou beauteous morn, serenely bright,
Now bursting glorious from the shades of night ;
And hail, thou Sun! whose warm and lively glow,
Diffuses joy above, around, below ;
Who flaming brightly in yon azure sky,
Proclaim'st the glory of thy God on high.
Oh! shed thy sweetest, but most brilliant ray,
On this his sanctified and holy day ;
Through the glad land thy cheering power dispense
To warm each heart, and rouse each grateful sense.
Then let all Nature with unerring voice,
And simultaneous accents loud rejoice ;
Wave thy triumphant tops, thou forests deep,
And in sweet peace, thou murmuring waters sleep !

Ye winds be still! but zephyrs, gently bear
Your Maker's praises to the list'ning ear.
And you, ye numerous tribes, to whom 'tis given,
To breathe the vital air of gracious Heaven,
In different ways your gratitude express,
And by your joy, your great Creator bless.
But thou, 'bove all, immortal as thou art,
Oh towering Man! now ope thine inmost heart;
For, chief for thee, Omnipotence hath blest,
And call'd this chosen day, " a day of rest;"
For thee allotted each returning space,
To cleanse thy soul by his redeeming grace;
To gradual break earth's low and sordid chain,
And clasp those links that bind to Heav'n again.

Every thing around seemed to conspire with the
happy state of my own mind. Not a breath of air
rustled the leaves, not a cloud overcast the blue
canopy of heaven; and the shadowy mists floated
gradually away before the king of light, leaving all
nature clear, cloudless, and unsullied. The cattle,
just sprung from their grassy couch, were lowing
in the meadows, the sheep were bleating on the
distant hills, and the little songsters of the grove
warbled in every tree, and poured forth their
richest and most melodious notes. The curling
vapour soon began to ascend from the chimneys of
the scattered cottages, and signified that their
humble inhabitants, unacquainted with the false

luxury which leads so many thousands to lose the most delicious portion of the day in a state of inertness, or of oblivion, were risen from repose. Where is the heart that all this union of peaceful happiness could not penetrate? Where the mind that its contemplation could not soften and refine? *My* bosom powerfully owned its involuntary and silent influence; and as my eye rested on the spire of the village church, as its top glittered above the surrounding trees, " Yes !" I exclaimed, " this, Oh Lord ! is thy day; and it is pure as the service to which it is dedicated. Thy hallowed name shall, in a few hours be pronounced in the accents of praise in yon simple edifice, and the noblest and most favoured of thy creatures shall acknowledge thy power, and declare thy goodness."

The motive which actuated my intended visit to this church, was that of a laudable curiosity, excited by an account that I had some time before received of its rector.

" Who," asked I, as I walked along the beach of a retired sea-bathing place in the south of England, " who is that pleasing and intelligent-looking young man whom I meet here almost every day, with an elderly gentleman who appears in bad health, and to whom he seems to pay the greatest attention ? There is something in his whole appearance which greatly interests me, and I cannot but fancy that it bespeaks a noble and a delicate mind." "You judge rightly," was the reply, "that youth indeed deserves your admiration. Born to affluence, his hopes were crushed, his prospects blasted, by one of those sudden and unforeseen accidents to which we are all more or less liable. He was an only child, and at the time that this misfortune occurred he was at the university, and being educated for the church. His mother, whose frame was naturally weak, could not bear up under the reverse which she experienced; and he hurried from his studies only to hear her last sigh, and receive her parting benediction. Another unexpected disaster deprived his father of almost all that he possessed; and as he could no longer be supported at college, he saw with grief that he must give up all idea of entering a profession on which he had fixed his heart. Without one repining word, however, he wrote to his uncle, a merchant in London, and requested that he would either take him into his counting-house, or endeavour to procure him some other situation; and then, concealing his disappointment in his own breast, he exerted himself to cheer and console his only remaining parent. His virtuous fortitude was not, however, doomed to be tried so severely as he expected. His uncle, a plain but a warm-hearted man, struck by that greatness of mind which could

make, without boasting of, its sacrifice, furnished
him with the means of completing his academical
education, at the same time inviting his brother-in-
law to spend some time with his family. Not,
therefore, having even the pain of leaving his father
alone and solitary, he returned with transport to
the university, and laboured with redoubled diligence to fit himself for his future situation in life.
One thorn, however, still rankled in his bosom,
and prevented peace from distilling upon it its
balmy sweets; so that though he was self-approved,
he was not happy. He had been long attached to
a very amiable young lady, and although he had
never openly avowed, his actions and his manner
had been sufficiently explicit for the eye of love;
and when he had a competence as well as a heart to
offer, he had resolved one day to proffer both for
her acceptance. But when he found himself
stripped of every thing, and dependant upon his
own talents for his support, he resolutely combated
his passion, and without even allowing himself a
last glance of her he loved, departed from her
neighbourhood. Soon after he had made this
courageous effort, he was told that she was engaged to another, and too late he discovered that
hope had hitherto silently cheered his heart, and
animated his exertions. Despising himself for
acting from any impulse but that of duty, he

tried to rejoice at this meaner principle being taken
from him, and at the prospect of what he trusted
would conduce to the happiness of his beloved;
but he dared not to inquire if his hope was well-
founded, and the constant struggle which he maintained with his feelings strongly affected his constitution.   When he had completed his studies, and
again presented himself before his father, his figure
was emaciated, and his complexion pale and sickly,
save that a hectic colour sometimes suffused his
cheek.   His parent, seriously alarmed, summoned
medical assistance to his darling son, and he was
recommended to seek a warmer climate, and milder
atmosphere.   In vain he represented his disease as
trifling, if not imaginary; and finding that his
father was resolved to spend his last shilling, rather
than neglect to follow the advice which had been
given, and averse to making a second application to
his uncle, he sought and obtained a situation as
tutor to a young nobleman who was going abroad;
and with many a tender assurance to ease the mind
of his parent, he accompanied his pupil out of the
kingdom.

Fortunately, his companion was possessed of a
kind and sensitive heart, and a compliant disposition;
and although he had been in a degree spoiled by
foolish indulgence, his propensities and inclinations
were by no means vicious; so that under the mild,

but wise guidance of his new governor, he made rapid improvement in taste and character, while he became sincerely attached to one who had opened to him new sources of enjoyment, and taught him to control and to respect himself.

One evening, when they were strolling in the environs of Nice, and watching the crowd of invalids who, tempted by the softness of the atmosphere, were riding or walking about, many, perhaps, in the vain hope of prolonging an existence which disease had already brought nearly to a close, a low carriage approached in which was seated a young lady, whose countenance exhibited a mixed expression of sweetness and melancholy, accompanied by another female, and with a gentleman walking by the side. The young nobleman felt the arm of his friend tremble within his own, and on looking up, he beheld his eyes steadfastly fixed on the group. But one object alone enchained him. The pale face on which he gazed was that of his lost Maria! With a powerful effort, however, he hurried on, but his irregular step, and agitated mien, proclaimed the intensity of his feelings. Unacquainted with the incidents which could alone explain the agitation which he had witnessed, Lord —————, with the most friendly interest, urged him to acquaint him with its cause, and unable to resist his importunity, he confessed the truth.

" And are you sure," eagerly inquired his hearer, the moment he had ceased, " Are you certain that your Maria is united to another?" " I cannot doubt it," he mournfully replied, " but I had never the courage to ascertain it beyond a question. Indeed, it is a subject on which I never allow myself to dwell; and we will even now drop it, my dear friend, for I still feel too acutely the weakness of my heart." His pupil said no more, but his pitying glances told him that he sympathized in his feelings, and their mutual friendship was from this moment doubly strengthened. As soon as they had arrived at their temporary mansion, Lord ——————— left his tutor under the pretence of inspecting some admired building, but with the real intention of ascertaining the exact situation of the lady whom he had seen. After making many fruitless inquiries, he at length discovered the lodgings of Maria, heard that she had only been a few days arrived at Nice, and above all, to his unspeakable delight, found that she retained her maiden-name. This was almost enough for his enthusiastic mind, and he was hastening back with his glad tidings, when he remembered that although unmarried, her hand might be still engaged. " But I will ascertain the fact," he resolutely exclaimed, and boldly calling at the house she inhabited, he announced himself to her family as the pupil of their former favourite. As he uttered this name, he bent his eyes on the countenance of Maria, and was delighted to behold it suffused with a tint of crimson. But when he proceeded to enlarge on the excellencies of his friend, and to describe his precarious state of health, her whole frame became violently agitated, till, unable any longer to control her feelings, she burst into tears. Her mother rose and led her out of the room, while her father explained to his visiter that her nerves were in so delicate a state, that the least thing hurried and discomposed her. But Lord ————— was not so easily deceived. He saw that the affection of his friend was returned, and, without farther preface, he unfolded to the astonished parent all that he knew of his feelings and resolutions, depicted his virtue in the most glowing colours, and ended by beseeching him to reward it by the gift of his daughter ; at the same time promising, that the moment he was of age, which would happen in a few months, he would present a living which was then vacant and in his gift, to his highly-esteemed tutor. The answer that he received exceeded his most sanguine expectations. " That man must be virtuous," said the gratified parent, " who could excite such a warm and disinterested affection in the breast of his pupil. But I *know* your friend to be so, and great was my sorrow when he left us without one parting word, although I thought I discerned his motive. I believe that my daughter may be brought to love, as she now highly esteems him, and I have sincere pleasure in this belief, because I think that in his keeping her happiness would be secure." "That is all I want, my dear Sir!" energetically exclaimed the warm-hearted youth, as he pressed the old man's hand; and then, rushing out of the house, he hastened to his friend. With as much caution as the impetuosity of his nature would allow, he related all that had passed, and then, readily participating in the eagerness of the lover, gladly accompanied him back to the mansion of his Maria. All that ensued may be easily imagined. Suffice it to say, that self-denial and constancy were amply recompensed, and benevolence reaped, as it always must, its own bright harvest of golden fruit."

" And *is* he married to his Maria?" eagerly exclaimed I, when this interesting account was concluded. " Not only so," replied my informant, " but contrary to all custom in these cases, this excellent young nobleman remembered and fulfilled his engagement, by presenting the living which he had promised to his former tutor; and he has thus not only secured the comfort of an amiable couple, but provided for his poor tenants a kind protector and zealous minister." " And where does the father reside?" asked I. " In the same village with his son. He has been lately unwell, and is come hither for change of air. Love and happiness, you see, have strewed the roses of health upon the cheeks of his young supporter, and doubtless, from his having experienced the pangs of sorrow, he now doubly appreciates the blessings he is permitted to enjoy."

From being made acquainted with the above circumstances, I felt the greatest pleasure in the anticipation of again seeing my interesting young stranger, and in a place too where I expected him eminently to shine. Merrily pealed the bells at the appointed hour; and as I listened to them from afar, they swelled one moment full upon my ear, and then died away upon the passing gale. As I proceeded along the road which led to the church, I perceived the comely matrons in their Sunday suits, issuing from the cottages on either side, some attended by their husbands, also in their best attire, and their children walking demurely by their side, or perhaps hand in hand before them, as conscious of their unusual finery, and as if their little bosoms were swelling with new-created self-importance. Each village belle, too, trimmed out in the gay apparel reserved solely for this favoured day, tripped forward with a gayer air than was observable on the six that had preceded it, more especially

M

if assisted by the friendly arm of some handsome
rustic in his holiday garb, and with a bunch of
flowers carefully stuck in the button-hole of his
coat.   One couple, however, whom I happened to
overtake, I could not help particulary remarking.
A pretty blushing maiden rested upon a youth
whose curling locks hung down beneath his hat,
and over his open forehead, and on whose countenance was depicted the most unaffected good-
humour.   Every now and then I saw him stooping
to whisper something into the ear of his companion,
and as if by mutual consent they sauntered behind
every one else, that they might, I supposed, make
their walk of rather longer duration.   A rose-bud,
stolen from his own gay *bouquet*, and placed
in her waist, with a pressure of the hand, and an
interchange of tender glances, were the silent expressions of love which they allowed themselves,
when it was at length, in spite of their wishes and
contrivances, perversely terminated.   But although
divided for a time, the maiden had not long to wait
before a ready hand was held out to her.   On inquiry, I found that they had been for some time
engaged to each other, and that on that day the
banns were published for the last time.   In a few
more they were to be united for life.

As I entered the church-yard I perceived it to
be thronged with people, who were formed into

groups and conversing together, before the last
bell summoned them into church. There I saw
five or six farmers, seated upon a flat tomb-stone,
or standing around it. Here, an assembly of their
wives and daughters, hearing or communicating
the events of the past week; while the old men,
seated in the porch, and leaning on their sticks or
crutches, were chatting (I conjectured) on ancient
days, and perhaps deploring the degeneracy of the
present race. The bell ceased, and in an instant
all were in motion. The church-yard was speedily
cleared, and the women and children, with reverence in their mien, entered the building, followed
by the men, taking off their hats, and stroking
down their hair with their extended palms.

Lowly was this little *House of God*, and simple were its ornaments; but methought, as I looked
down from its plain white walls to the cheerful
faces of its quiet congregation, there was more of
the spirit of meekness breathing within them, more
of the calm unassuming character which belongs to
the worship of Christ, than is discernible in many
prouder edifices. The young rector was already
in the reading-desk, and as I again looked at him,
I fancied I could trace in his very countenance, the
estimable son, the tender husband, and the pious
Christian; and it is when we hear the word of truth
pronounced by such a character as this, that it

strikes us with double force, and rouses us with tenfold energy. The Morning Hymn first called upon all to " awake " to praise and adoration ; and though no pealing organ sounded through the fabric, and though art had not trained the untutored voices which gave utterance to the strains, I felt a sweet sensation kindling at my heart as I perceived every mouth engaged in resounding the praises of its Creator. One soft, sweet voice, however, was every now and then distinguishable among the rest, and it was rendered, perhaps, more beautiful by the rudeness of the concert in which it joined. I turned towards the spot from whence it issued, and beheld an elegant female form standing in a seat beneath the pulpit. A veil concealed her features, but when she raised it from before them, her mild expressive countenance assured me that this must be Maria. At this instant, the fine bass voice of her husband was heard joining in the final chorus, and, as if inspired by the sound, the hoarse tones of the villagers were pitched to a still higher cadence. The strain at length ceased, and a solemn silence prevailed. The clergyman first broke this pause, with the blessed assurance with which our truly sublime Liturgy commences. His tone was clear and emphatic ; his manner calm, but earnest ; his look grave, but not austere. In the voice of brotherly affection, he pronounced the ex-

hortation which followed; and in one of deep humiliation, uttered that confession so befitting erring
and sinful man. He seemed not to be performing a
compulsory office, nor to be seeking admiration, or
courting applause; but he appeared to be the
humble and sincere Christian, conscious of infirmity,
devoted to the cause he had espoused, wrapped up
for the time in his religion and his God, and utterly
unmindful of the thoughts or the observations of
those around him. Too much impressed by the
solemnity of devotion to be carried away by unbecoming raptures, but too much warmed by its fervour, to be spiritless or insipid.

When he had concluded offering up petitions for
himself and his brethren to the throne of grace,
again was every voice raised in the praise of the
Eternal, and again the old and the young, the minister and his congregation, joined in one general
and grateful chorus. A plain, but excellent discourse followed; and I observed with delight that
every eye was turned towards the preacher, and
every countenance indicated the deepest attention.
Too clear to confuse, too short to fatigue,—it
reached the heart and convinced the reason. Little
adorned by the flowers of rhetoric, and unembellished by tropes or figures, it would not, perhaps,
have procured the meed of applause from the mere
scholar, or the severe critic; but of this its author

was not ambitious. He evidently sought to rouse his hearers to higher and nobler exertions of religious virtue, and to open the bosom of the sinner to the holy stream of repentance. An old man who was seated in the aisle, and who was bent nearly double by the weight of years, rose up when he commenced, and supporting himself by the back of the seat in which I was placed, seemed listening to him with the most greedy attention, as if afraid of losing a word of his discourse; and when he expatiated upon the delight and consolation which religion possessed the power of affording to those who were advanced into the last stage of life, and the light which it could shed even over the bed of death, methought the poor man's countenance kindled with a holy enthusiasm; and as I looked upon his furrowed cheek, I perceived a tear stealing silently down it. "Blessed young man!" I mentally exclaimed, "if thou hast done no more this day than cheered this aged breast, thou hast performed a work of mercy, which will be registered in the records of Heaven."

In the afternoon I again visited the little church, and soon after I had entered, I perceived with pleasure the rector's wife approach with her father-in-law, who, though apparently weak, was considerably improved in his appearance since I had before beheld him. After most of the congregation had dispersed, I loitered a few moments in the building, under pretence of looking at its simple monuments, but in reality to watch the gentle Maria as she stood by the side of her husband, inquiring after the health of some of his poorest parishioners, and giving advice, and promising assistance, to others. They, however, at last departed, and I prepared to follow them. Just as I was passing through the porch, the old gentleman, who was proceeding a few yards before his son and daughter, dropped his stick, and before he could stoop to recover, I had presented it to him. He courteously thanked me for my attention; and while he was making his acknowledgments, the Rector reached us, and politely and pleasingly addressed me, while I inwardly blessed the accident which had brought about for me this welcome introduction. We were all going the same way, as I intended to wander through the village, with which I was imperfectly acquainted; and discovering me to be a comparative stranger to it, he in the course of conversation offered to accompany me to the ruins of an antiquated tower, which were situated at a short distance, and which had often excited admiration. After proceeding some distance, therefore, we parted with our companions, and turned up a long and winding lane which led direct to our place of destination. Never did I more thoroughly enjoy a ramble, for every step was beguiled by the interesting conversation of the young rector. Well-informed, without being ostentatious, and open and easy, without display or affectation, his remarks were acute and sensible, and his sentiments correct, and breathing that spirit which should be infused in the breast of a Christian minister. When we arrived at the ruins, he pointed out to me, with the utmost enthusiasm, their most striking beauties, contrasted as they were by the rich and diversified scenery around them, and his ideas seemed to assume a new and quite poetical cast, as if in unison with the landscape.

" What a happiness it is," said I, " to possess a taste for the beauties which nature every where presents to us ; to love to contemplate her ever-varying features, and to discover in all her different appearances, something to admire, and something to improve." " Indeed it is," replied my companion, " and from my soul I pity those who can walk through this fair creation with their eyes closed to its inestimable productions, and their hearts insensible even to its silent charms, for they are deprived of a pleasure the most pure, and feelings the most truly exquisite, of which human nature is susceptible; and they are ignorant of what might often prove to them a relief from satiety, and a sweet refreshment after mental suffering. For my part, I consider yon hills, and meadows, and groves, as all speaking to me by a silence more expressive than language, and impressing on my bosom their own peculiar influence; and thus, while I wander amongst them, I seem as if I could hold a conversation with rocks, and woods, and streams, and they are companions who rarely satiate, and never disgust me."

As we returned from our walk, we met many parties taking an evening stroll; and, on entering the village, the cottagers were to be seen sitting at their doors, and enjoying a social chat with their neighbours. " I love to see the happy faces of these poor people on this blessed day," exclaimed the rector, " and cannot but wonder that any should be found who would desire to make it one of penance and mortification, rather than of innocent enjoyment. I once knew a gentleman who contended, that even after having twice attended divine service, and likewise employed a few hours in serious reflection, and religious study, it was improper to take a quiet evening walk; and thus, instead of wearing, as it should do, an aspect of holy cheerfulness, a gloom was cast over this day in his family, and his children learnt to dread it as a period of unwonted restraint, instead of being first taught to hail it as one of relaxation, and afterwards, from a higher principle, to bless it as one of peace and righteousness. Too many also, I fear, looking upon it merely as a day when there is an entire cessation of labour, seek for no purer pleasure, no greater good, than what *that* merely can afford, and therefore pass it in stupid and listless inactivity. How much better then to see them pursuing a recreation at once beneficial to their minds and bodies, than to behold them dozing away perhaps its concluding hours, or passing them in useless indolence!"

" Yes," I replied, " it is right and natural for all, (and more especially those whom long habit has rendered incapable of employing much time in study,) thus to vary the seventh day. But what shall we say of those hundreds, and many, alas! in the higher ranks of society, who profane and degrade the sabbath, by making it the witness of festivity and mirth alone, and who, neglecting it as the ordination of God, spend it as if it were merely the regulation of man."

" Of them, my dear Sir," he answered, " we can scarcely speak in too strong terms of reproba-tion; and so great is the evil which they cause, that all are called upon to prevent its extension by their advice and exhortation, and still more by their example. But as long as our youth, at an age when serious impressions are at best fleeting and transitory, are sent, without perhaps a directing and restraining guardian, to countries where this holy day is devoted to mischievous and exciting pleasures, we can hardly wonder that they should return disgusted with the more sober institutions of their own country; and that thus, habits of so dangerous and alarming a tendency should rather increase than diminish."

At this moment, we arrived at the parsonage, a pretty and comfortable-looking dwelling, in the rural decoration of which no pains or labour had been spared. A garden before it was filled with the choicest flowers, which perfumed the air with their fragrance; and the lower windows of the house, half hid by clustering roses, opened upon a green and sloping lawn. We passed through a veranda, up which the sweet clematis fondly entwined itself with the blooming woodbine and modest jessamine; and entered a small but elegantly furnished sitting-room, in which we found the old gentleman resting after his afternoon walk. " Where is Maria, my dear father," said the rector. " She is distributing her usual gifts to the children, my son," he replied. " Oh! true, and we will grace her levee by our presence, if Mr. —— has no objection;" and we accordingly passed to the back of the house, and entered a little orchard, where, under the shady branches of a spreading tree, were assembled a group of neatly dressed children, with a few women seated behind them, and the amiable Maria standing in the midst, with a book in her hand, and with a smile of encouragement playing upon her features. " My wife," said the rector, " is examining those children in their religious knowledge, and instructing them in some of their most simple moral duties. They form a small school, which she has herself established ; and, to excite emulation among her pupils, she distributes trifling rewards to those who, on inquiry, are found to have been the most good and dutiful during the preceding week. All the parents who choose, are invited to be present ; because Maria considers, that they may perhaps be themselves benefited by the scene, or at any rate taught how best to instruct and to manage their offspring." But the eye of the husband spoke more than his tongue chose to utter ; and, as he contemplated the form of her he best loved, it glistened with tenderness, with admiration, and with esteem. For my part, I thought I had never gazed on a more interesting picture ; for dignified virtue and simple innocence formed its most conspicuous and striking features. The lovely Maria looked like the prototype of kindness and of pity, in the act of enlightening the ignorance of childhood ; while the circle of youthful faces which surrounded her, were contrasted with the aged

countenances of their parents, as they observed all
that was passing with an eye of interest, and
watched their little ones with almost trembling
anxiety. I saw the features of one or two of them
lighted up with pleasure when *their* children were
praised for their good conduct, and rewarded for
their diligence, by the " rector's wife ;" while they
looked around them with a proud complacency,
which seemed to say, " It is *my* child that she is
speaking to."

When this pleasing task was entirely performed,
she joined her husband, and took his extended
arm, her eyes beaming with benevolence, and the
sweetness of her disposition depictured in her very
manner. " Oh, woman !" thought I, " thou art
often bewitching, but never art thou one-half *so*
attractive as when thou art doing a deed of charity, or cheerfully performing a virtuous action.
Thou mayest indeed allure the eye, or for awhile
fascinate the senses, but in no way like this canst
thou win the affections, or unchangeably secure
the heart."

The remainder of the evening was spent in agreeable and interesting conversation, which made me
speedily forget that I was almost a stranger , and,
with the most sincere regret, I beheld its termination at length arrive. It was delightful to me to
find a teacher of Christianity possessed so truly

with that pure and exhilirating spirit which he should endeavour to diffuse among his brethren. To see him the minister of peace, and the harbinger of good-will,—the consoler of the unfortunate,—the comforter of the wretched,—the refuge of the sinking penitent,—and humbly endeavouring to follow the bright example of divine perfection held out to him in the Gospel, by essaying to lead the sinner " from the evil of his way," and conducting him back to his offended God.

I took my leave. The newly-risen moon shed its chaste light upon every object, and millions of stars sparkled in the dark firmament above me. All nature seemed softened and harmonized by the silvery beams of the queen of night; and the lengthened shadows, the dark foliage, and the mild effulgence, which was cast upon the scene, all conspired to give a melancholy tinge to my ideas. " Yon lovely moon," I mentally ejaculated, " now irradiates *my* path. In a few years it will only serve to lighten the green sod that covers me; another people will walk in its beams; and those whom to-day I have seen active and buoyant with health and happiness, will, with me, be slumbering in the dust. Still shall the chaunt of praise resound in that holy edifice, and still shall that village be peopled by human beings; but from other mouths shall the same strain issue, and other forms

shall inhabit those humble dwellings. But, be it
so! let but hope, bright as this morning's sun,
illumine my departing spirit; and peace, soothing
as yon beauteous orb, cheer my fleeting soul, and
I will leave this scene without one sorrowing sigh,
and relinquish this mortal frame without one repining thought; for thou, Oh God! dwellest beyond those countless stars, and in thy presence is
' fulness of joy,' and bliss for evermore!"

A MARKET-DAY.

What's all this bustle,—all this noise,—
Of matrons, maidens, men, and boys,—
   Confusion, hurry-scurry?—
" Why, bless me, friend! 'tis *market-day*,
And now, what else, I humbly pray,
   Can you expect but hurry?"

WHO that has long lived in a country town, has not at some time or other witnessed, or participated in, the bustling importance of a market-day, made still more bustling if it happen on a Saturday, that day (if I may so term it) of shreds and patches, of rubbing and scrubbing. To the great and the gay, indeed, it is only one pre-eminently distinguished in the almanack of fashion; but to the tailor, the mantua-maker, and a long list of dependent classes, one of fagging completion and unceasing labour. But, be it what it may, the day of *buying* and *selling* is, to the farmer and tradesman, at any rate, one of the eventful and momentous periods of existence; and, to their wives and their dairy-maids, it comes laden with abundant stores,

but also abundant cares. It is certainly aware of
its own wonderful consequence, for it appears before us, even in full-blown plenteousness, and
seems to display its variety of riches with much
complacency and self-importance. But yet, me-
thinks, we should pardon its overweening conceit,
in consideration of its generous and merry aspect,
and surely there is something amazingly gratifying
to the pride and the self-love of man, in beholding
all the plenty of the land hoarded together for his
especial use, and to find himself courted to enjoy
some of the best productions of his country.

When I was some years ago staying for a time
at a small farm in the neighbourhood of a market-
town, I had an opportunity of seeing something of
the preparation made for this eventful day, and,
when it at length arrived, it was ushered in with
no inconsiderable clatter. " Jenny, you slut,"
vociferously called the honest farmer, " Jenny,
why a'nt you off. Come this instant, you hussey."
" Coming, coming directly, Sir," replied a shrill
female voice from above; and, in a few minutes,
the identical Jenny appeared, attired in her new
bonnet and gay lilac ribbons, and with the roses
of health profusely scattered over her plump cheeks.
" Now, Jenny," exclaimed her mistress, running
to her at the door, " remember you don't let the
butter go a farden under the price I've told you

N

It's a crying shame that you should ha' sold the other so cheap, when I'll make bold to say, there is not better butter in the whole county." " Very well, Ma'am." " And remember you count your eggs better. You gave four too many away last Saturday, and I'm sure they are all but given away as it is. Oh! and Jenny, be sure you dont forget that errand I gave you,—and remember the groceries,—and bring the ribbon, exactly the same as the pattern, or else I sha'nt have a bonnet to go to church in to-morrow,—and—." " And—the d—l, I think," impatiently exclaimed her husband, who had been upon the fidget during the whole of the notable lady's harangue, " you'll have the girl too late to sell her butter, and then where's the money to buy all your women's frippery, I should like to know?—Here, Thomas! Thomas! help this wench up." And Thomas, a raw lad of twenty, with a vacant grin upon his face, obeyed the summons, and speedily seated the fair maid safely between the two weighty paniers with which poor old Dobbin was laden. She had not proceeded many paces, however, when her mistress exclaimed, in an accent of grief and vexation, " Bless my life! I wonder what that girl's head's made of? If she has'nt forgot the flowers! Jenny! Jenny! come back,—come back, I say," and having succeeded in making her comprehend that she was to retrace her steps, she ran into the house, and returned with about a dozen bunches of flowers, all tied up in prim order, to attract the eyes of the town's-people. " Now, dont you go to put 'em there in the sun, and let 'em all fade, before you can sell 'em," said she, as she placed them carefully inside one of the well-filled paniers, and, with this parting admonition, Jenny again turned the head of her charger, and marched sedately away. " Saddle Captain for me directly, Thomas," muttered the surly voice of the farmer ; and while he was giving orders to his men, his wife went to commence her usual bustling career within her mansion. For my part, tempted by the beauty of the morning, I mounted my horse, and rode in the same direction as the blooming Jenny, whom I soon overtook, but found in such a piteous plight as would have moved the very heart of a stoic. Old Dobbin, possessing not the energy and dexterity of his youth, had stumbled by the side of the road, and being, like many of the biped species, unable to recover one false step, he followed it up with another, and, rolling in the ditch, actually deposited his fair cargo there also. But, alas ! this was not all ! The lid of one of the paniers, being ill secured, gave way, and out tumbled butter, eggs, fruit, pinks, and roses, in the most picturesque confusion.

N 2

Such was the predicament of the fallen maiden, when I, like a doughty and valorous knight, hastened to her assistance, and dragged her from her melancholy situation. When she felt herself again on firm ground, she looked first at her soiled garments with a deploring eye, and then at the pounds of butter which were soaking in the dirty puddle; while the inflamed and angry visage of her enraged mistress, rising to her imagination, still farther to depress her sinking spirits, she exclaimed, in the most imploring accents, while she blubbered forth the sorrow which oppressed her tender and over-charged heart, " What be I to do !——Mistress will a'most·kill me." " Oh ! no, said I, pitying her distress, " I will explain the accident to your mistress. And now, suppose you help me to release poor Dobbin from his miserable situation." And, accordingly, we together got the unfortunate beast out of the ditch, and set all his commodities as stright as circumstances would allow. Her fears of her mistress's displeasure somewhat allayed, again did the poor damsel survey, with a grieving countenance, her bespattered gown, while her wounded vanity was depictured on her features. Again, however, she set off on her ill-omened expedition ; and I, (with shame I confess it,) not being quixotic enough to remain longer by her side, and shield her from any farther danger, trotted forward for some time at a brisk pace. In my course, I overtook many other demoiselles, as plentifully stocked as the ill-starred Jenny, and passed innumerable vehicles stored with vegetables and fruits.

As I approached the town, I was aware, by the hum of voices, that the weighty business of the day had already commenced ; and when I had proceeded a little farther, I became sensible, by the delectable state of the road, no less than by the groups of farmers and four-footed animals whom I saw mingled promiscuously together in the blessed spirit of equality, of what it had already consisted. When I had passed this scene, and got fairly into the open street, I perceived the maidens of the mop and the broom busily employed at almost every door, in cleansing the pavement, over which, however, the country girls very unceremoniously passed with the baskets on their heads, leaving a dirty foot-mark at every step. When I had, with some little difficulty, procured my breakfast at one of the inns of the town, I proceeded on foot to that grand emporium of what are called " good things," the Market-place. On one side of a large open square were stalls, hung round with nicely-dissected animals, each guarded by rather a tremendous looking personage, clothed in the habiliments which are the peculiar distinction of his valorous race, and armed with a cleaver, the symbol of his authority over the unfortunate tribes on whom he exercises the power of life and death. Opposite to these were ranged, in " beauteous order," the graceful nymphs of the *cabbages*, whose vociferous and repeated calls of " Plase to want some pase to-day, Sir?—Excellent pase to-day.—Some good taters, Sir.—Ma'am, what be you plas'd to want?"—claimed the attention of those who would perhaps have dared to pass by without having recourse to these beneficent dispensers of the earth's bounties. Then, that every fastidious palate might find something wherewith to satisfy itself, there were pyramids of cakes, and piles of the school-boys' delight, *tom-trot* and gingerbread. All the fruits of the season were exposed temptingly to view; and toys, and crockery, besoms, and brushes, caps, and carters' frocks, with other articles of a similar description, completed the bountiful assemblage.

It may be readily surmised, that not a little noise was created, both by the purchasers and the possessors of those commodities; and it was, with some astonishment, that I heard it suddenly and almost entirely hushed. But the reason of this cessation soon became evident. That important and dignified inhabitant of a country place, the town-crier, approached, in blue, edged with flaming scarlet, while his ponderous head, and bushy locks, were surmounted by a huge cocked-hat, which added much to the grandeur of his appearance. And now, with his sonorous bell, he announces his approach, and bespeaks silence and attention. Many crowd round to listen to his important communications, and, with stentorian voice, and magisterial air, he tells them of the

" Lost, or mislaid,
Stolen, or strayed.

And then, with a proud gait, stalks silently away, to repeat his lesson elsewhere, unmindful of the eager questions and entreaties for farther information, which are poured upon him.

The ladies of the butter-baskets were accommodated in a building purposely constructed for their reception, and they were surrounded by a respectable number of very obsequious and silent attendants, in the well-trussed forms of geese, ducks, and fowls; while the gay productions of Flora were disposed amongst them, to add to their attractions. And here was bantering,—and wrangling,—and jangling!—Here was " confusion of tongues," and diversity of dialects!—Some debating the weighty question of the leanness or fatness, the dearness or cheapness of a goose.—Others, exclaiming against the badness of the articles, and some, with well-filled purses, disputing

the tender point of a penny-piece.   One gentleman
was particularly engaged in this interesting war-
fare, as he went about with eager eyes, and as
much celerity as the burden of flesh which he had
to carry along with him would allow.   A servant
who followed him seemed to be well laden with
individuals of the feathered species, and his master
occasionally glanced at his purchases, as if he were
inwardly contemplating the feast which they would
afford him.   I afterwards learnt, that he was not
only what is generally termed a *bon vivant*, but
that most odious and disgusting of animals, a glut-
ton; and therefore, doubtless, one of his highest
enjoyments consisted in what it appeared to do,
providing for the future gratification of his darling
passion.

Occupied in observing the motions of this self-
important being, I did not observe any one approach the place where I stood, until I heard a
sweet voice close to my side inquiring the price of
a delicate chicken, that lay upon the top of a basket, against which I was unconsciously leaning.
I turned at the sound, and encountered a pair of
the most beautiful black eyes I ever beheld, which
instantly fell before my gaze, only, however, giving
me an opportunity of discovering that their brilliancy was heightened by the contrast of a complexion, which, though inclining to the olive, was,

in the highest degree, clear and transparent, while a profusion of dark hair shaded the pale cheeks, on which not a shade of colour was visible. Her figure was light and fragile, her motions were strikingly elegant, and her hand, which was held out to receive her purchase, was so white,—so finely moulded,—it would have served as a model for a statuary !

All these discoveries I made in the course of a few seconds, though they cannot be compressed into an equal number of words; and I was only roused from my examination by hearing again the sound of her melodious voice. I did not catch what she said, but I observed a readiness to oblige —a look (as I fancied) of sympathy, in the woman who was serving her, which pleased me ; and my attention was still farther arrested, when the latter inquired, with a respectful air, if " the major was no better ?" " None, none, I thank you," replied her fair purchaser, in a melancholy tone, " I even fear that he is weaker;" and she was turning mournfully away, when another woman, who sat next to the owner of the chicken, with a hesitating, bashful air, stopped her, with " Ma'am, Ma'am, if you plase, I've brought you a few of our first strawberries, which I thought may-be your father would like. That is—if you'd be plas'd to accept them." A tear, the bright emblem of gratified affection, beamed in the eyes of her to whom this simple offering was tendered, as she took the strawberries, and, evidently, with a full heart, but with graceful courtesy, thanked their modest donor. Then gliding past me, she left the market, with an air of so much mingled dignity and sweetness, as at once to charm me, and to awaken the most lively curiosity. This feeling I could not resist the opportunity of gratifying. " Pray, who is that young lady ?" asked I of the butter-woman, at the same time following with my eye her who had excited the question. " Lord love you, Sir," she replied, " d'ont you know her?—Why, she's the talk of all the country, as one may say :" and, on my demanding the reason of her being so highly honoured, she gave me, with evident marks of pride at being the narrator of the story, much of the following account of the black-eyed unknown. It seemed, that a few weeks prior to my obtaining this information, a carriage drove to the principal inn in the town, out of which alighted a young lady, who immediately turned to assist an apparently feeble gentleman, when, at this critical moment, the horses, which had been left by the postillion, terrified by some sudden noise, started off at full gallop, and dashed with fury down the street. The young lady had mounted the step the better to assist her companion, and, with admirable presence of mind, she contrived to retain her place, until she saw the ungovernable animals hasten over the bridge, and then dart by a sudden turn towards the bank of the river which was entirely unguarded. Then, the pressing danger which threatened him who afterwards proved to be her father, gave to her slight form an almost supernatural strength. She sprung from her station,—threw herself before the horses, and finally succeeded in holding the infuriated animals by the bridle, until one of the many persons who had followed the carriage, and who fortunately arrived at this awful moment, lent her timely assistance. Then, exhausted by the astonishing exertions she had made, she pronounced only an emphatic " Thank Heaven!" before she sunk, totally insensible, upon the ground, in which state she was conveyed back to the inn. The moment that recollection returned, her parent was the first object that engrossed her thoughts. Starting from the arms of those who supported her, she wildly exclaimed, " Where, Oh ! where is my father ?" and not until the tender voice of that anxious father articulated " Here—here—and safe, my child," did a flood of seasonable tears come to her relief, and enable her gradually to rally her exhausted spirits. But she too soon discovered, that the frame of her beloved parent, before reduced by

tedious sickness, was dreadfully shaken by this
alarm. All night, the anxious daughter watched
by his feverish couch, but, in spite of all her care,
he was, the following morning, in so alarming a
state, that medical advice was procured, and, for
some time, even his life was despaired of. Nothing
could exceed the unremitting attentions which were
paid to him by his attached child, or the agonizing
grief with which she saw herself on the eve of being
deprived of (as it seemed) her only remaining parent. No thought of her own affliction, however,
subdued the strength of her mind, or was allowed
to palsy her exertions, but when life's almost exhausted flame again partially revived, and then
gradually continued to strengthen, the sudden re-
vulsion of feeling which she experienced, seemed
almost ready to overwhelm her. But the poor
invalid was still in a state of such terrible weakness,
that it was impossible for him to leave the town,
and all that could be done was, to move him from
a bustling inn to the quiet lodgings which he at
present inhabited, attended by a physician, who
proved a kind and valuable friend. As it was supposed, that this heroic maiden was a foreigner, I
learnt that a double share of curiosity had been
excited respecting her, and every one was anxious
to learn something of her story ; but all the certain
information that could be obtained, was, that her

father was a major in the army, and that he had been many years in India.

Having received a slight sketch of these particulars from my communicative informant, something, it must be acknowledged, to the detriment of her butter-basket, which meantime occupied a very small share of her attention, I inquired the name of the physician whom she had cursorily mentioned, half hoping he might prove to be one with whom I was intimately acquainted, and on whom I intended to call before I quitted the town. To my infinite satisfaction, it turned out as I desired; and not doubting that I should receive further information from him, I left the scene of business, in which I had been engaged in a manner very different to my expectations, and hastened to his mansion; and as he was particularly distinguished for an obliging disposition as well as a tender heart, I found no difficulty in inducing him to give me the following summary account, which he had received chiefly from his patient, whom he had attached to him by his kindness and attentions.

He was, he told me, the son of a country gentleman in the north of England, and being an only child, had been always the darling of his parents, the magnet to which their desires and hopes all pointed. His open, generous disposition, and naturally fine talents, long gladdened their hearts,

and constituted their pride; and too fondly for
their own future happiness did they nurture and en-
courage the daring and impetuous spirit that accompanied them. With the eager eye of an enthusiast,
he conned the page of history, and with a kindling
heart he dwelt on the patriotic self-devotion of a
Leonidas, or upon the exploits of an Alexander or
a Cæsar; or else with lively admiration perused the
lives of the Condés and Montmorencies of modern
times. With them he marched in imagination to
the fields of glory, and with them he mingled in
the strife and the din of battle. Such thoughts
and feelings having once taken possession of his
mind, he turned with disgust from a life of joyless
inactivity, or uninteresting study; and with a palpitating heart, and a flushed cheek, he one day besought his father to purchase him a commission,
that he might go and serve under the hero of England. The dismayed parent, shocked at a request
so little congenial with his wishes, condescended to
expostulate, but finding his son bent on following
his inclinations, he uttered an absolute and decisive
prohibition. The disappointed youth loved the
authors of his being with all the energy natural to
his character, and at first he sunk into despair,
without an idea of open disobedience to their commands. . But he continued to indulge in dreams of
military glory, and to fire his youthful fancy with

martial emulation, until schemes for the gratification of the passion that swayed his breast, gradually introduced themselves into his speculations; and becoming insensibly familiarized with the idea of deserting his parents, he finally resolved to enter the army as a private, and trust for future pardon to the indulgence of those to whom, until now, he had scarcely ever sued in vain. With a soul secretly revolting, however, from the clandestine step which he was taking, he left his home and proceeded to the metropolis, where he enlisted in one of the regiments which was shortly after ordered to the Peninsula. But before he quitted the land to which he owed his birth, and entered a scene of peril from which he might perhaps never emerge, he wrote a letter to his offended parents, fraught with expressions of penitence for his fault, of entreaties for forgiveness, and of hopes of speedily returning to them, crowned with honourable fame. His heart somewhat eased by this act of duty, he embarked with his gallant comrades, and although a few natural tears did bedew his eyes as he saw the white cliffs of his native Albion recede finally from his view, their gay light-heartedness, joined to the entire novelty of every thing around him, soon dried their source, and made young hope and joy again spring up in a bosom from which as yet they were seldom absent.

The toils, the continual hardships through which
our brave countrymen passed while opposing the fell
tyrant of France, are well known; and in these no
one partook with more enthusiastic zeal than our
young soldier, and he did not partake of them in
vain.   In a sharp skirmish with the enemy, he was
fortunate enough to save the life of a valuable
officer; and on two other occasions, he signalized
himself by such acts of determined bravery, that
he was gradually promoted until he obtained the
rank of major; and the martial spirit that stirred
within him seemed to presage that he was reserved
even for greater things.   But the soul that will
never shrink from danger or from peril, may
yet often be softened by woman's witchery, or be
penetrated by woman's charms, and his was to be
subdued by the tender sentiments of love.   In the
heat of a severe action, he wrested away the
weapon which was just pointed at the breast of a
wounded Portuguese, and he afterwards conveyed
to a place of safety the youth whom he had so opportunely succoured.   His sword-arm had been
rendered powerless, when his cowardly opponent,
taking advantage of his situation, was on the point
of sacrificing him to his fury.   Grateful to his pre-
server, the young Portuguese besought him to accompany him to his home, which was only at a
short distance from the spot on which the army was

encamped; and then, sweetly was he repaid for his humanity, by the blessings of parents whom he had saved from severe affliction, and the silent tears of gratitude which flowed from the eyes of an attached and only sister. It was a moment of ecstasy such as he had never experienced; but alas! beneath the smiling surface lay dangers the more alarming from their concealment, and as the beautiful Victoria knelt by the side of her wounded brother, her soft eyes, moistened by the tear of gratitude, and her lovely features, animated by an expression of deep-rooted thankfulness, the shaft of love entered his heart, and its subtle poison diffused itself through his trembling frame. But he knew it not; and, admitted at all hours into the bosom of a family whom he had redeemed from misery, he daily discovered new graces both of mind and person, in the fascinating Victoria. At length, however, he became aware that his soul was possessed by her image, and he felt that his future happiness depended upon her. The flame was mutual; gratitude gave place to a warmer sentiment in the breast of Victoria, and the secret first disclosed by the tell-tale eye, was soon confirmed by the faltering voice. But while yet a child, she had been affianced by her parents to a young man of noble family, who was soon expected to claim the hand of of his promised pride. " I can never, *never* be

O

yours, Theodore," said the weeping Victoria. "My father's word is sacred, and I must be its victim." "Impossible!—you—*you* be sacrificed to so absurd an agreement! Perish the thought! Oh! for the first time in my life, I am tempted to wish that I were not a wandering soldier, that I might dare to ask you to fly into these arms for refuge—to seek your home upon this fond bosom." "Theodore," replied she, with solemnity, "mine is a woman's heart, but it could bear much when it was near its lord. I cannot plight my faith to any but thee. *With* thee, I should be happy amidst toil and hardship—*without* thee, I should be miserable if surrounded by all the vain pageants of earthly grandeur. I will follow thy fortunes, I will share thy fate. If I remain, my father will enforce the fulfilment of his promise, even at the expense of a child he loves. If I depart with thee, his honour will be safe, and he will in time pardon, and even bless us "——

"But, my sweet Victoria!" replied the astonished lover, his eyes sparkling with rapture at this testimony of the devotedness of her affection, "Dost thou remember that thy husband would be the inhabitant of a camp—a rough soldier of fortune, without even a single comfort to offer thee—liable to the vicissitudes, open to the dangers of war? No, dearest—it is not I who can take advantage of

such generosity. It is not I who can expose that
tender and beauteous form to toil, and perhaps to
sorrow "———

"And could you better bear to see me the bride
of *another*, Theodore?" said she, looking with beseeching earnestness in his face. "Alas! I can fly
from, but I cannot resist the authority of my
father. Fear not for me. No murmur, no sigh,
at any temporary suffering shall grieve thy bosom;
I will greet thee with smiles in thy tent, as if thou
wert returning to thy palace. I will stimulate and
not weaken the martial bravery that is employed in
defending the sacred soil of my country. I will
help to trim thee out for battle; nay, I will send
thee forth to it with an unblanched cheek, nor shed
one tear till I am alone with my weak sorrow.
And if," she added, the exalted and enthusiastic
expression of her countenance giving place to one
of agitation which she found it impossible to conceal, "If thou *should'st* be taken from me, I can
but return to a home which will not then be shut
against me, and I shall have had the unspeakable
satisfaction of having soothed thy last hours, and received thy last sigh. Theodore! you cannot refuse
me?" "Good God!" exclaimed the painfully agitated lover, "and can *I* have inspired such a love
as this? Oh, Victoria!" he continued, folding her
tenderly in his arms, "thou hast indeed conquered

me—be it as thou wilt;" and unable to articulate another syllable, he rushed from her presence.

One peaceful night, when all nature was sunk into a holy repose, and scarcely a sound disturbed the universal stillness, the silvery beams of a resplendent moon lighted the devoted pair in their perilous desertion of the paternal mansion; and before the morning sun rose in the east, their destiny was united in the sacred bonds of religion, and with the British army they were leaving the native province of Victoria, whom her husband consigned to the care of a wife of one of the officers with whom he was acquainted, and who more leisurely followed the troops.

With unabating affection, with never-ceasing fortitude, was this heroic female for months the constant companion of the man she adored; and though bred up in the soft lap of luxurious indulgence, she submitted with unfailing cheerfulness to the severest privations. She seemed like a ministering angel hovering over the destiny of her Theodore, her bright eye always shining upon him with the same tenderness, her cheek always hailing his approach with a speaking flush of joy; and her delicate hands appearing most willingly employed when administering even to his slightest wants. He was at length wounded in battle, and *then*, in that hour of dread, did her soul burst forth with full effulgence.

With all the melting sympathy of woman, she watched over his bed of suffering, listened with forced calmness to his half-stifled groans, and with her sweet voice, and encouraging smiles, softened his anguish, and inspired him with some of that patient endurance which characterized her own meek yet powerful nature. At last he rose from his couch of pain, with increased gratitude for her affection, and admiration of her fortitude; and as he glanced at her pale cheek and increased form, a pang of mortal anguish seized his soul at the thought of what she might soon, perhaps, have to endure, without parents, and without a home. But fortunately, before that time arrived, his regiment returned to its own sea-girt island, worn down by fatigue, and grievously reduced in numbers; and as he again touched its happy shores, not as he had left them, destitute and alone, but ennobled by fame, and blest in the possession of a heart which it was his delight to think his own, he felt that while he deserved to have been the victim of justice, he was chosen as an example of transcendent mercy.

Much, however, was his happiness embittered by the misery which Victoria experienced at the total silence of her parents, to whom she had repeatedly and urgently written. "But mine will love her," thought he, "they must admire her for herself, and adore her for her attachment to their son, and it shall be the study of my whole life to cherish and deserve her." He took her to them—knelt with her at their feet—and was clasped with her in their sheltering arms. Oh, happiness! how brief are thy moments! how perishable, how evanescent is thy power!

The trying period so dreaded, and yet hailed by the fond husband, arrived; and with maternal pride the happy Victoria placed a smiling babe within his arms. But alas! the seeds of consuming disease had been planted by fatigue and anxiety in the tender form of the mother. A decline, rendered doubly terrific by its frightful rapidity, tore her away in her spring-time of happiness, just when the forgiveness for which she had yearned had arrived from her still doting parents.

" Theodore," articulated the dying wife, " my husband, lament not for me. I am now as blest as this world can make me—were I to live, I must doubtless partake of its cup of misery. A gracious Providence has visited my faults with gentle retribution, indeed—I am grateful, I am resigned.—Be thou so too, my love, and I shall be more,—I shall be happy !"——

And so he seemed, while the eyes of her he loved yet lingered upon him, for did she not say, " It would make her happy?" But when they were closed by the impressive seal of death, he gave way to all the bitterness of his sorrow——to all the distraction of his grief.

With the restlessness of misery, he again left his home, and consigning the fruit of his short-lived joy to the care of his parents, sought in a foreign clime, and surrounded by new scenes, to banish the memory of the past. Twice, however, in the course of fifteen years, did he hasten from India to fold his little daughter to his breast, and to dwell with a melancholy satisfaction upon features which seemed to recall to life his lost Victoria; while his tender caresses during these visits, and his kind admonitory letters, added to the narratives of his exploits, which were early impressed upon her memory by those about her, gave birth to feelings of mingled reverence and affection in her susceptible bosom, which seemed too mighty to admit of any other equally powerful, and consequently this was the animating emotion of her soul. And when this idol of her innocent heart returned at last to her, with an enfeebled frame and shattered constitution, he seemed in her eyes possessed of even an additional interest, and devoting to him both her time and thoughts, she gradually let in upon his bereaved spirit the warm sunshine of happiness. He took her with him into Portugal, and with parental pride presented her to the friends of her he never ceased to lament; and then, after retracing with her the scenes of his transient felicity, he bore her back to England, and was journeying towards the north when the incident happened with which I was first made acquainted.———

When my kind-hearted informant arrived at this point in his narration, to which I had been listening with the deepest attention, I started, energetically exclaiming, "He cannot, he will not die! It is not possible that two such hearts should be dis-united!" But my enthusiasm was instantly checked by the answer of an ominous shake of the head, which too plainly denied my conclusions, and my heart bled at the thought of the affliction which probably awaited this affectionate daughter. "Yes," said my companion, "I fear that his span of existence is now short; and when I sometimes behold his lovely child bending over his pillow, with strong anxiety depicted in every feature, I feel that I would give worlds to avert the too evidently impending stroke. But how little, indeed, my friend, can we understand the mysterious ways of Providence. This, however, we *do* know. These objects of our pity are in the hands of infinite Wisdom. And with regard to her who most needs our sympathy, we may hope the sorrow which endureth during her night of trial, will be followed by a morning of succeeding joy. Heaven is righteous and merciful, and its decrees are just and wise."

Impressively he pronounced these words, for he was a man of strong religious feeling, and innate piety; and I, affected by what I had heard, and disinclined to enter upon any less interesting topic, took my leave, and hastening along the streets, disgusted with the scene of bustle which had before served to divert me, again mounted my horse, and returned pensive to my quiet lodgings, ruminating on the events of the morning, and surveying in "melancholy mood" the disastrous scenes presented by human life—its cares, its sorrows, and its vicissitudes, coming at last to that conclusion at which all must arrive, when meditating upon such a subject——that it is at last but a short journey in the progress of which we must expect to meet with accidents and crosses, and that instead of loitering on the way to lament and bewail them, we should hasten with increased speed towards that "land of promise" which is to reward us after our toils. The same decision has been made, the same sentiment pronounced a thousand times, but I confess that the well-known truth, though it must have met the approbation of my reason, never sprung so directly from my heart, as when I pictured to myself the interesting being whom I had so lately seen, an

orphan, desolate and bereaved, with all the gay
visions of youth clouded by misfortunes, and its
dreams of felicity dissipated by mournful reality.

But her destiny, though obscured, was *not* per-
manently darkened. The loss she was doomed to
sustain did indeed press heavy on her soul, and
long did the deep shades of melancholy cast a gloom
over her naturally joyous mind. But the heavenly
Protector who watched over, provided for her new
sources, and opened for her new prospects of a
happiness which, though mixed and imperfect, was
as great as is usually allotted to mortality.

" Yes," have I since often repeated to myself,
when looking back upon her early trials, " my
good friend said right,—sorrow *did* ' endure for
a night,' but joy was allowed to ' come in the
morning.' "

HUMBLE VIRTUE.

Mock not the poor man's useful toil,
  Deride thou not his humble fate;
But from his mild contentment learn
  A lesson for thy loftier state.

A LITTLE cottage stood apart from the rest, in the
midst of the village which I had just entered.   Its
roof was composed of thatch, out of which peeped
a little opening which was intended for a window,
while one of rather larger dimensions served to enlighten the lower room.   Four well worn steps led
up to the door, and by their side was a rudely-con-
structed seat, on which reposed an old man with
his feet placed upon the second stone, and his two
hands laid upon a strong oaken stick, on which he
rested his aged head.   An old great-coat, well
patched, and " telling tales of many a hard-spent
day," was his upper garment, and on his head was
a round broad-brimmed hat, from underneath which
flowed his hoary locks in unrestrained luxuriance.
His back was a little bent by time, and his brow

was furrowed by the years which had passed over it, but he seeemed even yet to possess some of his ancient vigour, and his keen grey eye was still lighted by the fire of his youth. "Good morrow, Gaffer," said I, "what you are in your old place, I see—how goes it with you, my friend?" "I thank you, master, I hav'na any thing to complain of," replied he, raising his head at my salutation; "to be sure, this rheumatis plagues me, and my old legs wont do me much service now; but what o' that, Sir? we must all be old once, and I thank God ha' many blessings to be thankful for." "And how is your daughter, Gaffer?" said I. "Why, Sir, she is but mighty middling. She's been at death's door since I see'd you, Sir—but the Lord thought proper to restore her; and though the doctor's fees have run hard on us, yet it might ha' been a deal worse, you know, Sir; and now her's getting something like about again, we must na' grumble." "You are very right, Gaffer," replied I, "to look at things in such a cheerful light; and how is your son, who used to live in yonder cottage?" "Ah, Sir!" answered the old man, wiping his eyes with the back of his shrivelled hand, "that be a sad story. He fell from a cart, Sir, and broke his leg; and he was ill a long time, but he died at last, Sir, and his young head was laid low before his poor old father's. But however," continued he, rising from his seat, " we must na' grumble. He was a good lad, and I'd rather see him die than do ill, and the Lord knows best what's good for us, you know, Sir." " He does, indeed, my old friend, and I wish every body would think as you do, and then there would be far less misery in the world." " Why you know, Sir, if the storm blows we canna stay it by striving against it, and we must na' arraign the deeds of Providence; besides, Sir, I ha' many comforts still——though I *often* miss poor Bill," added he, brushing away the unbidden tear which rolled down his cheek. " He used to come after he had done his work, and give me his arm, and lead me up the village. Ah! he was a good lad." " Well, Gaffer," said I, equally touched by his sorrow, and his pious resignation under it, " take *my* arm. This fine evening, a walk will do you good, and I want to have a little chat with you." " Heaven bless you, Sir, you be a deal too good;" and with this declaration, the old man took my offered arm, with a look half doubtful, half grateful, at accepting so distinguishing an honour. " You see, Sir, my leg has never recovered my last fit of rheumatis, or else if it was na' for that, I could walk a many miles yet — and indeed," added he, stretching up, and waving his shrivelled arm, as if in proof of his assertion, " I could do a good day's work yet, an'

they would let me; but instead of that, I am
obliged to see the youngsters taking my place,
while I rest my old good-for-nothing bones in idle-
ness." I soon found that the post which I had
occupied was not a little conspicuous, although I
was indebted to my companion for the notice that
I excited, for every one knew old Gaffer. He was
the sire of the village, and all his neighbours looked
up to him as almost to an oracle. He was often the
arbitrator of their little disputes, and the solver of
their difficulties. "But Gaffer says,"—would often
decide a warmly-agitated question, and his opinion
was asked in all cases of emergency,—as when any
misfortune happened to the cattle, or when the
crops would not thrive. Thus he might be called
the little monarch of the place, only that instead of
possessing outward marks of sovereignty, he reigned
in the hearts of his people, and guided their conduct, not by laws, or through ministers, but simply
by his sentiments and advice. His old seat by the
door of his cottage might be considered as his
throne, round which his subjects assembled in an
evening, to talk of present affairs, and hear the tales
of other days; and never were a monarch's words
listened too with such charitable and unscrutinizing
attention as were those of my friend Gaffer.

As we proceeded up the village, every one whom
we met made some sign of recognition to the old

man. Some nodded and smiled, others doffed their hats, and some ventured to add an inquiry after his health, while I could hear the women, as they peeped after us from their doors, saying, "Look, there goes Old Gaffer; God bless the good gentleman that's a leading him." When I had taken my humble friend back to his cottage, and reinstated him in his former place, I bent my steps homewards, meditating on the display of true contentment which I had just witnessed. "This poor man," said I to myself, "has had many trials. In his youth, he obtained a scanty subsistence by the sweat of his brow, age has now rendered him incapable of labour, and he is dependent upon the kindness and the exertions of others. Yet does he not repine at his situation; and even, while lamenting the sorest of his afflictions, the loss of a good and affectionate child, he acknowledges that he has still cause for gratitude and thankfulness; while thousands, who are rolling in wealth, and surrounded by luxuries, are yet mourning over imaginary evils, and magnifying the most insignificant losses into real misfortunes." After fixing his attention upon it, perhaps for months, and making every exertion to obtain the desired object, my Lord —— is disappointed of some expected favour, —Alderman *Turtle* is cursed with a tardy cook, who keeps his dinner sometimes five minutes be-

yond the specified hour, and allows him time to
devour it in imagination before he can feast upon
it in reality.—Young Dashington has waited *four*
days for a new pair of boots, which his " rascally
shoemaker" promised him should be completed on
the first, and, moreover, the " impudent scoun-
drel" has the assurance to demand the payment of
his last account,—while Lady *Racket* had the
agony of hearing, that the rooms of her rival, Lady
Francis Vere, were crowded to excess at her last
rout, with people of the first fashion, while her own
were very thinly attended,—and Miss Seraphina
——— has not been able to procure a morsel of de-
cent rouge for the last twelvemonth ! Oh ! the evils
and calamities attendant upon this imperfect and
sublunary existence ! Would that I had the pencil
of a Raphael that I might delineate ye in the deep
and striking colours that ye deserve, or possessed
the sublime language of a Young, that I might
convey some faint idea of your greatness ! But,
alas ! so much genius is denied me ; and even were
it not, I with grief confess, that so obtuse are my
visual organs, that I often cannot even discern the
miseries which are endeavoured to be pointed out
to me ; or, perhaps, when I am told to behold
dark heavy clouds in the horizon of life, I distinguish nothing but a faint mist, which entirely disappears as I continue steadfastly to gaze at it. But

I humbly acknowledge my own stupidity, while I admire the quick sight of many of my fellow-mortals, and congratulate them on having advanced so much farther in the laudable progress of discovery.

Two years after the little incident which I have been relating had taken place, and when I was again staying in the same neighbourhood, I thought I would pay another visit to poor old Gaffer, and see what change this period would make in his aged frame; and I accordingly set off towards the village which he inhabited. As I passed some of the cottages at its entrance, I was surprised to see the inhabitants standing at their doors, and gazing with sorrowful looks, as if in expectation of some approaching spectacle. When I turned a corner which obstructed my view, I soon beheld the cause of this unusual excitation. A funeral procession was advancing towards the church. The clergyman walked first. Then appeared six men, bearing the last remains of some fellow-creature in its narrow bed, and a few mourners succeeded, followed by a long string of the villagers, who seemed all, more or less, to participate in their sorrow. I turned to a little girl who stood beside me, and demanded whose funeral I beheld. "Oh! Sir," she answered, with the utmost simplicity, gazing at me at the same time with unfeigned astonish-

P

ment, " doesn't you know as poor old Gaffer's
dead ?" " Dead," I repeated, gazing at the coffin
as it passed by me, " old Gaffer dead !" surprised
and shocked, I scarcely knew why, at an event,
which was indeed so natural, and so little to be
lamented; but I was just hastening to see, and to
converse with (I believed) a living creature ; and
there was something that chilled my heart, to think
that the few planks which I beheld contained only
his cold and inanimate form.   Impelled by an irresistible feeling which possessed me, I followed the
mournful procession at a little distance, and when
it had reached the place of interment, I drew sufficiently near to see the concluding ceremony.   Our
beautiful and sublime burial service was read with
impressive dignity by the officiating minister, and,
as I listened to the solemn words, I could not help
wondering how they could ever be pronounced with
that air of cold indifference with which I have
known them uttered.   I am indeed convinced, that
were this ceremony performed with the devotion
and the feeling which it demands, it could not fail
to produce a great effect upon the minds of almost
all who attend it ; and, of the crowds who sometimes rush to it, merely for the purpose of gratifying idle curiosity, many would return impressed
with a strong feeling of awe which might perhaps
lead to thoughts and reflections of a tendency the

most salutary and beneficial. If all the ministers of the Church of England did but consider this as one of the opportunities given them for furthering that great cause, for which they ought so unceasingly to labour, they surely would never (as some few unhappily do) perform this fine service in so careless and irreverent a manner that the religious depart from the scene disgusted and dismayed, and the profane with still harder hearts and lighter principles. But to return from this digression. When the coffin had been lowered into the earth, and " dust" consigned to its parent dust, the clergyman addressed the assembled group, in apt and forcible language, expatiating upon the blameless life of their deceased neighbour, and exhorting them to imitate his industry and integrity, while they learnt from his fate what a blessing attends the last moments of the sincere Christian. When he had concluded, the villagers dispersed in different directions, some proceeding to their houses, others collecting in groups to talk over the life and the actions of the deceased, and to lament his departure from amongst them ; while I, affected, as it is impossible to avoid being, at beholding a fellow-mortal consigned to that last home at which we all must finally arrive, walked pensively back, with my heart tuned to grave and melancholy reflection. " Thus has terminated this

poor man's blameless career," thought I, " and
what is now the distinction between him and the
greatest potentates who have succeeded him on the
stage of life.   Heroes, and statesmen, and artists,
who have in turn excited the wonder and the admiration of mankind, are reduced to the same
level with this honest peasant.   But were *their*
struggles after glory,—their toils for attaining or
preserving power,—or their labour for fame in the
ages which should succeed them, as acceptable in
the eye of the Almighty, as this man's contented
mind, which asked not for more than was given,
but cheerfully enjoyed the little of which he was
permitted to partake?   Thy wearied limbs," I
mentally exclaimed, " are now at rest.   Thy task
is finished upon earth, and thou art gone to receive
thy hire.   Let not the rich or the great despise thy
humble tomb, or scoff at thy silent fate, for thou
liest as peacefully in thy grassy sepulchre, as they
will do in the most splendid mausoleum; and the
humble stone that pillows *thy* head, is as soft as
the glittering marble which emblazons *their* fallen
grandeur."

FASHION.

We set up an idol in our hearts, and then, first blinding our Reason, worship it with fond idolatry.

MAN proudly boasts, that as he is created lord of this lower sphere, so he is free and independent of every earthly power; and that he breathes the pure air of a liberty which no other creature can invade. And yet, while thus plainly acknowledging the blessings, and claiming the triumphs, of freedom how often does he voluntarily divest himself of one of the highest gifts which he possesses, and actually place around his neck, with his own hands, the yoke of Fashion, the shackles of custom, or some other badge of a state of slavery, equally odious and oppressive. He defies even his fellow-men to rule over his actions, and revenges himself on those who shall dare to usurp what he deems his rights, while, at the same moment, both his soul and body are perhaps under the guidance of an imaginary power, to be moulded as that power shall please to direct.

While I was one day musing with grief upon the strange inconsistency which is thus observable in the human mind, I fell insensibly into a train of thought, which ended by Fancy's usurping the throne lately occupied by sober reflection, and swaying her sceptre with so unlimited a power, that I knew not for some time that I was subjected to her dominion. She suddenly transported me into the midst of an immense building, or kind of hall, at the upper end of which, appeared a large and apparently festive group, to which numbers were every moment hurrying with inconceivable speed. Curious to know what could excite all this haste and eagerness, I also followed the general example, but before I had advanced far, I was stopped by a grave but intelligent, and, on a minuter inspection, a very pleasing looking personage, who styled himself *Reason*, and who commanded me to go no farther, under dread of being infected with the general mania which prevailed. "Here," said he, "you may remain in safety, and behold clearly all that passes beyond; whereas, if you proceed, your visual organs will be quickly obscured by the magical arts of the idol which yon fools are so servilely worshipping, and you will not be aware of your own dangerous situation." "And who," said I, "is this wonderful creature who seems to hold so astonishing an influence over that throng

of human beings?" "Her name," said he, " is
Fashion; she is the offspring of Vanity and Error,
by whom she has been deeply initiated in all the
wiles which are necessary to introduce her to the
human heart; and there you may see the effects of
her diabolical skill. The young and the old, the
rich, the learned, and the great, are alike bowing
prostrate before her, and watching her every motion with the most intense eagerness. See what
rich and splendid offerings they lay before her!
What sacrifices they offer at her shrine! while all
is spurned haughtily away, as unworthy of her
notice and acceptance, and fresh supplies are continually demanded, and as continually ceded.
With what expert industry does she constantly
vary the gay and parti-coloured dress in which she
is arrayed! and how anxiously do her votaries
observe and copy all even her slightest movements!
Some, you see, glorying as it were in the extent of
her influence and *their own* blind credulity, while
others seem borne passively along with the general
tide, content that they go with others, without
examining the intent or termination of its course;
and others again are struggling to escape from the
impetuous violence of the torrent, though so weak
and feeble is their resistance, that few indeed
really succeed in their purpose." " And what is
it," said I, in great amazement, " which can thus

retain them in their present situation, even against their own inclination?" "Against their own inclination," replied my informant, "nothing indeed can retain them, for that is too powerful even for the domination of Fashion. But the fact is, that *that* is still possessed by her, although a transient view of my figure has partly dispelled the illusion under which they have been labouring; and if they would survey me steadily, and crave my assistance, with a real desire of obtaining it, they would soon acquire sufficient strength to approach me nearer. But, unfortunately, my rival yet offers charms to their imaginations, and as I may not enter farther into her precincts, I must wait until they first exert their own endeavours, before I can render them any effectual assistance." At this moment, I saw, approaching the group before me, a venerable old man, whose appearance greatly interested me, and whose evident feebleness excited my commiseration. "What!" exclaimed I, involuntarily, "and is he too infatuated with this syren?" "Yes," answered my companion, "my power has been for some time diminishing in his mind, and now I fear it will be totally annihilated; but I will make one effort for its re-establishment," added he; and he beckoned the old man towards him with a mixture of authority and entreaty. The latter started,—paused for an instant,—but then, as if with determined desperation, quickened his pace, and hurried on, although with tottering step, to the object of his search. " He is now beyond my reach," said Reason, with a melancholy voice, " and he, who has for sixty years followed my dictates, and been ruled by my decrees, is now going willingly to immolate himself at the shrine of that unpitying sorceress. Behold the transformation which she has already wrought in him." Directed by his words, I, who had just been watching some other victims, followed his glance, and to my utter amazement, beheld the reverend and respecable figure which I had just been admiring, changed into one of the most ludicrous appearance. In return for the sacrifice which he had made, Fashion had completely remodelled his dress and manner, and, instead of the grave countenance on which I had before gazed, and which suited so well with his years, I beheld one which was forced into a thousand grimaces, and aping the smiles and the gaiety of youth, which contrasted strikingly with the wrinkles which time had made in his forehead. His person had undergone as complete a metamorphose as his face, and presented a curious mixture of helpless infirmity and assumed lightness and ease. I sighed with pity at this instance of the degradation of all that is most to be admired in the human character, and, turning away, directed my attention to another, although equally painful, object. A young and beautiful maiden appeared, conducted by those who should have made it their study to have preserved in her mind that purity and shrinking delicacy which Fashion delights in undermining or destroying,—even by her parents, —to that altar at which they had themselves been wont to sacrifice. It was her first appearance in these hateful but fascinating regions, and she tripped on in blushing modesty, unconscious of her error, beaming in the radiance of beauty, of hope, and of excited expectation. Her young fancy appeared charmed with the outward seeming of gaiety which prevailed, and she was soon lost in the midst of the crowd which opened to receive her. I stood for some time pondering on what I had witnessed, when suddenly she again appeared in sight, but, alas! what a cruel change had taken place! The roses of health which once flourished on her cheeks had given place to the false colouring of art. The bright but timid glances of her eyes were superseded by those of conscious loveliness seeking for praise and admiration; and the animation which once played naturally around her features was succeeded by the fixed smile of a constrained levity, which Fashion teaches to her children. The full beams of truth were no longer visible, and the veil of retiring delicacy was cast aside. She was, in fine, become a slave in the glittering but deceitful train of Fashion.

"How wretched," exclaimed I, " is the fate of that poor young creature! How much is she to be pitied!"

"Yes," replied my instructor, " and yet, after such a warning of the pernicious counsels and gifts of Fashion, thousands will rush into the same snare, and experience the same fate. The youth too, who should be the pride and the ornament of their country, and the supporters of its power and its liberty, have bowed under the same rod, and are enervated by the same control. Honour, patriotism, principle, and even religion, are exchanged for frivolity, dissipation, and licentiousness. But behold yon gaping crowd in the distance. How eagerly they are endeavouring to follow those whom birth or wealth have enabled to get first in the race! and how comic are their imitations! how ridiculous the laborious efforts which they employ! and how unceasingly they struggle to obtain the few scattered remnants which Fashion throws from her contemptuously, when it suits her capricious temper to change the taste and colour of her dress! Oh! Man, Man! what a satire thou presentest of thyself! Of thine own weakness, of thine own laxity of principle, and degeneracy of feeling!"

Reason uttered this apostrophe with so much earnestness, and in so emphatic a manner, that *Fancy* was forced to drop her veil, and give place to the sober garments of reality.

———

THE AFFLICTED FAMILY.

What is life?—a scene for ever shifting;
A landscape of a thousand varying hues,
And what is earthly bliss?   An empty shadow,
When nearest gained perhaps farthest from our reach;
Ever pursued, but sliding from the grasp,
To mock the daring hopes of him who sought it.
  But even here below there is one good,
Real,—substantial,—which once gained, all else
Will vanish from the sight, or seen in Truth's pure mirror,
Shew to the eye, vain, frivolous, and mean.
Its name,—Religion!

MUCH has been said of the changeability of life, and the instability of all human things.   These are subjects which have engaged, for successive ages, the attention of the philosopher, the poet, and the moralist; on which much has been indeed already said, although much also, perhaps, remains to say. Arguments are, however, useless to prove what is never disputed; but hacknied truisms seldom produce any very considerale effect, because what is universally acknowledged and established is made

little subject for reflection; and we want something, not to convince our minds, but to make our
sensations correspond with our avowed opinions.
One single incident, happily chosen, and drawn
from nature itself, will be more likely to answer
this purpose than volumes of the most abstruse argument; and it is with such a view that I would
now delineate a scene, upon which I myself often
dwell with peculiar though melancholy pleasure;
and then reversing the picture, place before the
reader a representation of others which have succeeded it.   And while he gazes upon even my imperfect sketch, I think his heart, as well as mine,
will be fully impressed with those sentiments which
should, indeed, be always firmly stamped upon it :—
that, as all that surrounds us is transitory and perishable, we should not fix our thoughts or our hopes
upon what is so constantly insecure; and that to
expect the enjoyment of perfect happiness upon
earth, is only to court disappointment.

  Well indeed can I remember how blest was once
the happy mansion in the soft vale of Riversdale.
The smile of peace gladdened its aspect; the
sound of joy reverberated on its walls; and the
hand of elegance had decorated it with all that
could conduce to comfort or to beauty.   Its white
front peeped through the many-coloured trees that
fondly embosomed it, and before, its little verdant

lawn sloped down towards a stream which ran murmuring between its flowery banks, while the green hills rose gradually on every side, as if to shield and protect the habitation of innocence.

Three lovely maidens bloomed in this spot, where nature seemed to have thrown together some of her choicest works to vie with, and to emulate each other. A fourth was also there; but alas! her cheek had been long tinged with the hue, and her eye had been dimmed by the effect of sickness. Never could she taste that feeling of inexpressible happiness, and almost intense delight, which gladdens so many of the buoyant hours of youth. Never was her mind irradiated with those gay visions of hope and expectation which belong exclusively to that joyous season. Happily, however, although she was a constant she was not a severe sufferer, and her quiet unrepining spirit led her to submit to her fate with calmness, so that her temper was never ruffled, nor her spirits painfully depressed. She could not but sometimes, indeed, look around her, and feel conscious that those of her own age and sex were animated by pleasures which she was incapable of enjoying, and gay with emotions which she could not experience; but still she murmured not. She saw them happy, and that was sufficient to make her so likewise; she saw them smile, and she smiled in sympathy; and if she *did* sigh for herself, the sigh was breathed in silence and in secrecy. Her family thus saw her always contented, though not gay, and they felt that they had great cause to be thankful that her mind had not participated more closely with the grievous weakness of her frame. The gentle Penelope, the amiable and open-hearted Elizabeth, and the lively Ellen, all united their efforts to charm and to gratify her; and their brothers, as well as the excellent parents with whom Providence had blest them, encouraged and seconded their endeavours. All were, indeed, knit together by the bonds of love; and though the characters which composed this happy family differed essentially from each other, the utmost concord and equanimity prevailed, because the desire of communicating pleasure, and the habit of self-denial, were common to all; and surely the most beautiful sight which this world is capable of producing, is a *family at unity with itself!*

The sire of the group was one whom all respected, and many loved. He was like the hoary mountain, whose grey summit towers by itself in majestic dignity, and on whose fostering sides the young vines luxuriantly spread and fondly cling. He was esteemed by the virtuous, and adored by the poor and the distressed, to whom he was an able protector; but there was a something which marked his countenance that would put vice to the blush, and make impiety tremble, and even the timid would shrink before his penetrating eye, until his smile of benevolence encouraged and re-assured them. The partner of his bosom was possessed, perhaps, of quicker and more ardent feelings, but she was one whom to have once seen was not sufficient. Nature had stamped her in no common mould; and the spectator was first struck by the more bold and the commanding features, and afterwards charmed by the milder lineaments of her character. She was enthusiastic in the cause of virtue and religion, and devoted to the service of her Creator. She regarded many things as trifles which might appear important to others, but if they happened to touch the interest or the feelings of those she loved, they then appeared in a new light; and little was necessary to engage the services of one by whom self alone was disregarded.

Such, then, was the circle which assembled round the cheerful hearth, in the mansion of Riversdale, when I, happy in the thoughtless gaiety of childhood, was the plaything and the darling of the group. Caressed by each in turn, I was stationed on the knee of the smiling old man, played off a thousand childish tricks with his amiable daughters, or romped with wild and unrestrained glee with their kind-hearted brothers. Thrice happy were

Q

the days in which each hour teemed with somewhat that was joyous and pleasing! Thrice-blessed the family, who, alive to the value of all the good which was allowed them, displayed their gratitude by contentment and cheerfulness, and while they fully performed their several duties, remembered

" That to enjoy, is to obey."

But, alas! fleeting as beautiful was this scene. Like a summer's sun, whose pleasing radiance reflects for a time its own bright aspect upon those who walk in its beams, but too soon disappears in the gloom of evening,—awhile it flourished in all its loveliness, and then vanished for ever.

With regret, and many a fond adieu, I left the spot in which my heart had experienced so much delight ; and my bosom throbbed, as I thought that I would one day prove to those whose kindness had caused it, that, young as I was, I knew both how to appreciate their goodness, and to be grateful for their attentions. But that unspeakable gratification was, in part at least, denied me. Happiness is truly said to be no plant of this world's growth. It requires a far richer soil, and a purer atmosphere; and if to-day we behold it endeavouring to expand to view, to-morrow we shall see it sickly, drooping, or withered.

Quickly, indeed, the peace which I had witnessed was but too rudely dispelled. An accidental misfortune first deprived this inestimable family of the affluence to which they had been accustomed, and the heart of the father sunk at beholding the children on whom it doated reduced to comparative indigence. They indeed tenderly but earnestly strove to soften the violence of a blow, which they saw had fallen on him so heavily, and, by redoubled cheerfulness, endeavoured to convince him, that they themselves were not depressed or unhappy at the change, while, for their sakes, he struggled to subdue the anguish which rent his soul. But the dart was rankling within him which could never be plucked out. The parent was too powerful for the man, and the cold and silent grave alone closed upon his sorrow!

Deep and severe was this stroke to the widow and the fatherless! Grievous the wound that it inflicted on those who had been so little smitten with the rod of affliction! The mansion of delight was transformed into the mansion of mourning! The vale of joy presented alone the cold desolation of sorrow! But still—still were both dear to that stricken family,—for they were the witnesses of their infantine sports, and their childish pleasures: and this was the scene which had been illumined by a father's smile, and a father's approving eye.

They were not, however, even allowed the melancholy satisfaction of dwelling among the mementos of their past happiness, and in them retracing those sweet feelings which they knew that they could never again experience. Riversdale was no longer for them; and a few months after they had consigned the ashes of its beloved master to their last sad home, they bid adieu to a spot which had in their eyes been consecrated by his presence.

Only a short space was allowed them to recover from what seemed even yet as a stupifying dream, or a frightful vision; and then another bitter drop was infused into their already overflowing cup of sorrow. Ellen, the fair, the intelligent, and the high-minded, whose buoyant spirits and light-hearted gaiety, had, in former times, preserved amongst them one continued flow of pleasurable emotions, drooped, like a faded lily, under trials too great for her endurance. With ardent feelings, and a keen relish for enjoyment, she had not, perhaps, that calm stability of character, which is the best calculated for bearing calamity with firmness; nor let those who have not sorrowed like her, sneer at what they may term her weakness, but remember, that the susceptible heart, just expanding under the genial influence of hope, and maturing in the balmy atmosphere of social and domestic felicity, is ill-prepared to sustain unmoved the desolating blast which at once destroys that beautiful paradise in which it had so peacefully reposed.

Poor Ellen's form shrunk, and her eye became divested of its brilliancy, for the elasticity of happiness had deserted the one, and frolic and merriment no longer lighted up the other. At length, the agony of her mind produced corresponding effects upon her body. A frightful fever seized her frame, and preyed upon her intellects. Her affectionate sisters sat by her bed-side, and while they watched her wild and haggard countenance, and listened to the ravings of her distempered fancy, thought that they could almost lie down and die beside her, for life was robbed of all its brightest charms to them. Reason and recollection returned at length to the expiring maiden, but returned only to light the last narrow passage to the tomb, and to disperse the gloomy shades which sometimes hover over the bed of death.

During all her illness, and even when she had breathed her parting sigh, her mother, strong in her religious principles, remained like a rock, against which the wind may blow, and the waves may dash with their utmost violence, in vain. Her eyes rested on Heaven, and therefore her heart could not faint upon earth. The husband, whom she loved,—the child, whom she cherished,—were both gone ; but she trusted that they were only flown to *Him* from whom they came, and she murmured not that he reclaimed his own.

With her three remaining daughters, she retired to a still smaller habitation than the one she had some time occupied, and endeavoured, by introducing them to a new scene, and to fresh objects, to divert their minds from dwelling upon the melancholy events with which they were chiefly engrossed. For her gratification, they strove to acquire some degree of serenity, and each was repaid for her individual efforts, by observing among the rest a slight resumption of their wonted cheerfulness ; and thus is virtuous exertion ever rewarded, either by being crowned with the success which it desires, or by the satisfaction which even itself can impart to the breasts of those from whom it springs.

Alas ! they were speedily called upon to make efforts still greater and more painful. The handsome, the mild, and the elegant Elizabeth, whose sweet and winning manners, and whose highly-cultivated mind, and admirable sense, had always ensured her the esteem and the affection of those who knew her, had attracted the eye, and captivated the heart, of a youth, for whom she acknowledged an equal preference, and, in the hope of beholding her happy, her family felt a ray of returning gladness steal over their hearts. But futile are the hopes, and uncertain the prospects, of mortality. Her health had received an injury from the scenes which she had witnessed, which, though not immediately apparent, was not the less fatal in its consequences. Some secret poison appeared to be gradually diffusing itself through her veins, and sapping the very springs of life, until at length it was evident that exhausted nature must sink beneath the pressure. Six months after the departure of her sister, Elizabeth was no more!

And could a woman's heart bear up under such an accumulated load of grief? Yes; for that heart was dedicated to its Maker, and it dared not to repine at His decrees. It could still utter, therefore, the language of resignation, and pray for that succour which is never denied to the righteous.

But deep was the grief of him who had centered his every hope of earthly felicity in the form now faded in death. As he gazed on the closed eyes that had looked upon him only with love, and the stilled mouth that had so lately breathed words of consolatory tenderness, I say not that he could mutter " thy will be done." No, he felt as if his very soul was gone. He thought that misery was his only remaining portion; and it was long before one ray of comfort broke upon the darkness of his spirit, and much longer ere peace, with healing on her wings, hovered over and soothed him with her benignant influence.

Poor Penelope too, who, in Elizabeth, lost a faithful sister, and her most beloved friend, felt that she was comparatively lonely on the earth. But her lot in this world was more prosperously cast than that of her she lamented. While her heart was yet sensible of its void, and softened by its sorrow, it was more than usually susceptible of the tender influence of love, and to an object who deserved them, she yielded her affections, and, after some time, her willing hand. She has never repented of her choice; and, the wife of the man whom she esteems, and the mother of a blooming family, she often indulges the painfulness of retrospection, that she may become still more sensible of her own comparative felicity. Her fate thus affords one bright gleam to cheer the gloom of my melancholy picture, and on which the eye can rest with unabated pleasure.

The widow then, and the feeble Maria, were left to comfort and to support each other during the remainder of their pilgrimage; and, in many respects, they were meet companions, for their feelings and their ideas were in unison, and each could truly sympathize with the other. Together they sought consolation at that spring from whence alone it can effectually proceed. Together they explored those " hidden mysteries," the knowledge of which " leadeth unto life," and together pursued that holy but narrow path, by which alone the traveller can eventually reach the goal of immortality. It was indeed apparent to all, that neither could be very long the tenant of this world, for though the mind of the mother remained unshaken, her constitution was evidently shattered, and it was only hoped that " death would not long divide them." The wish was accomplished; the course which they had together trodden, nearly together they completed. One still soft evening, after they had been for some time talking on different subjects, their conversation gradually assumed a more serious cast, and the poor Maria, in adverting to her own lot, expressed her sincere gratitude to Providence, for having so darkened her prospects upon earth, as to make her justly estimate its scenes and its pleasures, and lead her to fix her thoughts upon those of a brighter and more durable nature. " My dear mother," she added, with strong and remarkable emphasis, " I feel somewhat within me, that tells me that I have not suffered in vain. I know that I am sinful, but I know also that ours is a *God of mercy*." As she uttered the last words, her countenance assumed an aspect more than usually serene, and the fire of unwonted animation kindled in her eyes. Her mother turned, and gazed on her. In another instant, the hue of death spread over her face;— the body remained, but the spirit had fled for ever!

"I am thine, Oh Lord! do with me what thou seemest good," exclaimed the bereaved mother, as she looked upon the lifeless corpse. "It is not for me to limit the period of my sufferings, but Oh! do thou graciously enable me to bear them."

Such was the language of a Christian; and it is in a season like this, that the mind which is strengthened and illuminated by the divine influence of religion, shines with its brightest and clearest lustre. In prosperity, it may charm by its kindness, and delight by its benevolence; but, in adversity only does it put forth the greatness of its strength, and towering above all sublunary things, soars onwards in its own high tract with unwearied steadiness.

It was this spirit, and this only, which supported the lonely mourner through the few weeks which yet remained to her, and when she felt that her end was at length drawing nigh, and that her trying probation was about to cease, she hailed the long-wished-for moment with unspeakable delight, and with trusting faith, peacefully gave up her soul into the hands of its Creator.

The corn was perceived to be ripe, and the sickle

of mercy was sent to gather it from the ground. The remembrance of the fulness of its perfection, alone remains to animate the diligence, and excite the admiration of those who beheld it in its beautiful ripeness; but if there is hope in heaven, again will it appear at the great day of universal harvest, in more than earthly freshness, to be planted in the courts of its Maker, and dwell in his glorious presence to all eternity.

SCANDAL.

***

Oh! holy Truth! why take thy rapid flight,
And leave us wand'ring here in Error's night,
  Or Folly's sickly glare ?
Why, chaste Simplicity, dost thou depart,
And with thee pure sincerity of heart,
  Ye guides of virtue, rare ?

***

" My dear Lady Wormington, you look most charmingly this morning," said Mrs. Smoothly, to the lady who had just entered her room, to kill one of the tedious morning hours, by recapitulating all the tales of scandal which she had picked up the preceding day; " I dont think I ever saw you look better in my life, I protest you are becoming quite young again." " Yes, that she really is," drily observed the malignant Mrs. Venom, " she bears all the gay colour of youth ;" at the same time glancing from her cheek to the bright rose-coloured dress which she wore, (and which vied with each other in the brilliance of their hue,) to give point to her remark, so that all but the person who excited it, might be aware of its latent meaning.

The object, at which this sarcasm was aimed, was indeed one of rather ludicrous description, to those at least who do not think, that as every thing is now made to appear different to what it really is, youth should assume the importance of age, and age should imitate the dress and manners of youth. She had evidently passed the " grand climateric" in years, and her form began to bend under their weight; but rouge was resorted to, to conceal the wrinkles of that barbarous enemy— Time ; the gayest plumage decked out her sinking frame, and she proceeded onwards with a tripping movement, which was meant to indicate the possession of unabated strength and vigour. When she had thrown herself back in her chair, in a position which she meant for one of easy elegance, she turned to the lady of the mansion.

" My dear Mrs. Smoothly, have you heard of this shocking affair for poor Mrs. Belford. It is really dreadful—they say"—" Oh dear, how delightful! then you know the particulars—pray tell us all about it,—I depended upon hearing every thing from you,—I was only told that Mr. Belford had eloped with a beautiful opera-dancer, (whom I declare I myself heard him openly admiring the other day,) and that his wife had been in fits ever since. To be sure, poor thing! it is a terrible thing that he should have made so public a business.

of it, though, as Mrs. Venom and I were agreeing just now——" "For my part," interrupted the latter lady, impatiently, "I think she affects a great deal of goodness, and all that nonsense, for herself and her husband; and she is rightly punished, for pretending to think him so superior to every body else; and, as for him, such over-righteous people are always hypocrites."

"Well, but let us hear all about it, my dear Lady Wormington," again repeated Mrs. Smoothly, drawing in her chair, and placing herself in an attitude of attention.

"Lord bless me!" cried Mrs. Venom, just as the lady, in answer to a request so much in unison with her own wishes, was beginning her narrative, with the self-importance of a person about to disclose some valuable piece of information, "why, here is actually Mrs. Belford herself. Bless me! I suppose she has cast off her modesty and tenderness, and is coming out in a new character, now that her lynx-eyed husband has flown away."

"Let us get the truth from her own lips," exclaimed Mrs. Smoothly; "my dear Mrs. Venom, do you question her, for you know I have such delicate feelings," whining out the last words to give them their proper effect. "Ah!" returned her sneering companion, in a tone of pretended sympathy, "it is a melancholy thing when these troublesome appendages of human nature are allowed to be thus always stumbling in our way. But I really thought you had got over such a weakness. I positively gave you credit for a more masculine understanding," seconding her remark at the moment with a penetrating glance from her searching eyes. "Why, I assure you," retorted the other, striving to conceal her anger at the malevolence of her more open though equally ill-natured companion, "I assure you I have endeavoured to overcome my naturally too susceptible feelings, but they will sometimes—" "Come to your aid, when you want to condole with your friends on their misfortunes. True, and here is this poor deserted—Dear me! she seems to bear her loss with amazing equanimity."

As she uttered these words, a lady, apparently about thirty years of age, simply but elegantly dressed, and with an air of mingled dignity and sweetness, entered the room.

"I am truly glad to see you," exclaimed Mrs. Smoothly, hastening to meet her, and in her most silvery tone, and sympathizing manner, "I feared, after your sad—However, it delights me to observe, that you have so much greatness of mind—" "Oh!" added Mrs. Venom, "you can scarcely conceive what deep commiseration has been felt for you by this amiable creature," darting a malicious glance towards Mrs. Smoothly, " she is actually a pattern of benevolence."

" Upon my word," said the lady who was thus addressed, at the same time looking unaffectedly surprised, " I cannot even imagine to what you allude. I have not the slightest idea why I am an object of pity."

" Well, now really," answered Mrs. Smoothly, " this is treating the thing as it deserves. It is indeed an event which may ultimately tend to your happiness."

" What event can you mean ? To what is it you allude ?" said the new comer, with a still more perplexed countenance ? " I beseech you to explain yourself."

" Why, it is not possible that you should not have heard that Mr. Belford——"

" Nay, allow me to tell the whole story," eagerly interrupted Lady Wormington, " I had it from the best authority, and as poor Mrs. Belford must be acquainted with the particulars——"

" You will tell · them with characteristic truth and precision," drily observed Mrs. Venom.

Lady Wormington, happily unconscious of her meaning, immediately began her narrative ; part of which she had certainly heard from others ; but her fertile brain had successfully toiled to fill up the vacant spaces, so that it was rendered complete in all its parts and bearings, and wonderfully proved her own unexampled sagacity.

During this recital, the countenance of Mrs. Belford underwent a considerable change. At first, a contemptuous smile alone was visible; but when she discovered, that not only the malicious eye of scandal had pretended to detect the alienation of a heart which she gloried in feeling was hers, and hers alone; but that its busy voice had even rumoured, that the husband she adored had forsaken her, and deserted the pure and upright principles which had ever actuated his conduct, her fine eyes shot for a moment a glance of unsuppressed indignation, and her cheek glowed with the tinge of resentment. But the fire of the one was quenched, and the hue of the other was softened, before Lady Wormington had completed her story, and only an air of offended dignity remained. She then rose from her seat.

" It is perfectly evident, Madam, that you are totally unacquainted with the character of my husband, or you could not, as you appear to do, believe him capable of an act so every way unworthy of him. Fortunately, I have had so many proofs of his excellence, that the *particulars* which you have troubled yourself to communicate have not even the power to excite a moment's jealousy, more especially as the fact which they are intended to

R

prove can hardly be established, since Mr. Belford is now at the door, and perhaps, indeed, I had better summon him to prove his own identity."

So saying, she rang the bell, and despatched a message to her husband, while Mrs. Smoothly poured out numerous protestations of her sorrow that such a shameful report should have been mentioned, and her happiness at finding that it was so completely without foundation. Lady Wormington looked towards the door with an anxious glance which seemed to express an ardent desire to pass through it, and Mrs. Venom put on a smile of malicious incredulity. Their suspense was ended in a few moments, by the entrance of a fine commanding-looking man, with a countenance which, usually remarkable for the benevolence of its expression, was now impressed by a degree of sternness and gravity. The truth, indeed, was that he had remained below in the carriage because he was aware of the character of those persons who were to be usually met with at the house of Mrs. Smoothly, and while he despised, he yet could not restrain his anger at its meanness.

"Edward," said his wife, "pray come hither: the good-natured world will have it that you have found out that I am not perfection, and therefore," and a slight colour passed over her cheek, "that you have sought it elsewhere, leaving me, I suppose, bathed in tears of anguish, or something of the kind; and so," added she, smiling, " I think I must display you about by my side for some time, and I begin my exhibition here."

" An excellent place, Emily, depend upon it. Indeed, if I mistake not, you may end it here also, as these ladies," glancing round him while he spoke, " will, I have no doubt, have the goodness to correct the mistake under which the *good-natured world* have so strangely laboured, although I am fully aware that this is a piece of information which from its nature will not travel so fast as that which has preceded it. And now, my identity being established so as to put even the doubts and surmises of scandal to flight, we will if you please depart."

Mrs. Belford readily obeyed her husband's signal, and returned with him to a cheerful home, which was never darkened by discontent, or polluted by the noxious vapours of malice; leaving the amiable trio to cogitate over what had passed at their leisure,—Lady Wormington to lament over the stop thus put to the further extension of the news, to the circulation of which she had generously dedicated her whole morning—Mrs. Smoothly to conceal her chagrin at Mr. Belford's rebuke, under expressions of rapture at finding so " shocking a thing " had never happened,—and Mrs. Venom to indulge her splenetic disposition in inuendoes against all her acquaintance.

Alas! I fear there are many Mrs. Venoms, but still more Mrs. Smoothlys in this world of hypocrisy, in which truth and rudeness are too often deemed synonimous, and sincerity is denominated insult. Unfortunately, also, it is not only in the highest regions of fashion, where an artificial language is unreservedly employed, and artificial sentiments expected,—that that openness and candour which must always form the most beautiful constituent of a character is neglected; nor is the pure garment of truth laid aside merely that scandal may have a wider range, or that malice may enjoy a richer banquet. It is perhaps more injuriously, though more innocently, neglected, for the specious dress of politeness, or the more glittering ornaments of compliment, among those who do not profess themselves the votaries of Fashion; so that even the nearest friends are sometimes wearing to each other an assumed habit, and, for the modest sincerity of a virtuous spirit, is often substituted a shame-faced fearfulness of offending.

I mean not, however, to depreciate that genuine politeness which springs from a kind and generous heart. This is one of those softeners of existence which tends greatly towards making the path of life smooth and easy, and prevents many of the rough particles, and opposing qualities, which are mixed in the composition of human nature, from rubbing against each other, and producing by friction the most disagreeable consequences. But there is another species, bearing indeed the same name, but differing essentially in its real qualities. The one is the offspring of nature,—the other is the production of art. The former leads its possessor to avoid wounding the feelings, or exposing the frailties of others, when duty does not demand it. It makes him strive to diffuse general good-humour and complacency, and avoid unnecessary harshness and asperity. It is very nearly akin to, or perhaps deserving of the title of benevolence; and benevolence is not only the brightest ornament of human nature, but one of the proudest boasts of Christianity. The latter, although it may on the first glance appear to produce very similar effects, is, in reality, but the disguise of envy, ambition, or hypocrisy, put on to conceal the real form of its wearer, by engaging the eye of the spectator to rest on its seducing colours, without desiring to penetrate beneath them. Like all counterfeits, however, it ceases to please the moment that it is detected; although such is the force of example that others will still continue to imitate what they yet acknowledge to be no longer agreeable.

And why is it, that under various forms and

denominations, such a regular system of hypocrisy is established and carried on in the world? May it not be most generally attributed to that overweening pride which cannot bear aught that tends in any degree to its mortification, and which, for its own gratification, will even condescend to the employment of subterfuge?

I suppose we may likewise trace to the same source, that love of pomp and of display which in the present age is so strikingly conspicuous, and which leads hundreds to set up and to support pretensions to which, in reality, they have no right.

To second some of these numerous claims, that admirable invention, *puffing*, is resorted to as an excellent auxiliary; and with this, every body knows that, among other things, our newspapers (and many more publications which kindly acquaint us with what is good for our mortal frames, and what beneficial for our minds) constantly abound. There are *puffs* of as many and various descriptions, as the commodities in whose service they are employed; and while these are working their way, their author stands behind the curtain, slily watching their progress, and observing their effect.

To answer the same end, also, fine *epithets* of all sorts are in great requisition, and are exceedingly useful as a sort of *gilding*, which may be resorted to in many emergencies, for the purpose of concealing defects and inconsistencies which would otherwise be inconveniently prominent and conspicuous. I believe, indeed, that honest *John Bull* is altogether ashamed of the homeliness of his mother-tongue; and he is, therefore, very busy importing into his country shreds and scraps of other languages, which (being but a bungling contriver,) he engrafts upon various parts of his own, without greatly heeding whether the seams or the stitches be visible or concealed; so that I suppose it will at length become like a "coat of many colours," in which the original one will be scarcely perceptible.

Indeed, it is wonderful to consider the new creation, which has, through this and similar means, sprung up in these our days. We have now superb titles for objects of almost every description, so that not only new things are provided, but old ones are garnished up with a fresh and more splendid name, and palmed upon the gaping multitude for novelties.

I sometimes amuse myself in thinking that we want another Linnæus, not indeed to arrange the natural, but to classify the artificial world; for really, the various species which compose it are not only so rapidly increased, but their titles are so multiplied and changed, that it becomes worthy the art of some such profound genius to unravel this "mighty skein of words," and reduce the whole to some kind of regular system, so that we may be enabled to distinguish what is at present so complicated and confused.

After all, however, and great as would be the ability requisite for such a task as the above, I know not if nearly equal ingenuity be not displayed in the art of substituting sound for substance, and appearance for reality. True, man is now seldom obliged to toil in advancing things towards perfection, for the *liberality* of the present age is satisfied if he employs his inventive powers in making them *seem* as if they were doing so; but then, I think all will confess that this must employ no small portion of finesse and skill; and if he be not so completely master of his art as to prevent its being sometimes discovered that all is not what it appears to the eye, or sounds to the ear, he must then employ his dexterity in heightening the deceptious gloss which he finds so valuable an agent, and which can scarcely indeed be so glaring as to offend either the taste, or the visual organs of the beings of this our generation.

THE FAREWELL.

How sweetly shines soft Charity's blest power
Amid the darkness of affliction's hour,
Shedding fresh light upon life's dreary road,
And cheering penury's cold and bleak abode.

On a dull, gloomy morning, in the dreary month of November, I once found myself mounting the steps of one of those vehicles termed stage-coaches, abounding in every part of merry old England, whose inhabitants no longer, like their worthy ancestors, remain as a fixture in the town, or even perhaps in the very house, in which they were born and bred, without stirring from thence above once, perhaps, in the space of twenty years; but are whirled about at the rate of ten miles an hour, to any part of the kingdom to which their fancies may direct them, at the simple price of the lives of some hundred of poor unfortunate horses, for whose health or comfort lordly man seldom thinks it necessary to provide, excepting when either his purse or his vanity are concerned in their preservation; and *then*, indeed, the quadruped is raised almost to an equality with the highest of the class of bipeds, or even engages a share of his thoughts and attention which any one of the latter would probably in vain attempt to obtain.

As soon as the door was shut, *Coachee* had smacked his whip, the emblem of his dominion over his four-footed subjects, and I had made myself, what is so happily expressed in our own language, by that unrivalled word *comfortable*, (that is, had wedged myself closely into the only vacant corner that appeared, and fastened one of my hands in the loop placed upon the side of the coach for the accommodation of those restless members,) I looked round to see what individuals of my own species divided with me the sovereignty of the confined territory which I at present occupied.   And first, my eyes naturally explored the opposite point, where they rested upon a tall, robust, and military looking figure, which showed so few indications of even approaching age, that it was not until I had traced the furrows which appeared in the face above it, that I could guess that at least seventy years must have rolled over it. But although the features were somewhat marked by time, the fire of youth still glowed in the countenance, and the grey piercing eyes emitted glances of such stern keenness, that they required the sort of smile,—the fixed expression of benevolence, which was settled about the mouth, to qualify their repelling effect. It was as if a cloud hovered above, but a bright sun-beam played beneath it; and I afterwards found, that its mild effulgence was universally diffused, when the contraction of the brow was softened and relaxed by conversation. There was a commanding dignity in his manner, the effect of which not even the bluntness and freedom of his speech could entirely remove; and his *tout-ensemble* led to the idea of his being a veteran of the ocean, an opinion afterwards confirmed by the coachman's addressing him by the appellation of admiral. By the side of this then, on the whole, prepossessing figure, sat a little, mean, diminutive, looking personage, with a sharp aquiline nose, twinkling black eyes, and a facetious grin stationed upon his face, which, being thus always at its post, could never be behind-hand, when any occasion might seem to require its aid. He appeared remarkably fond of hearing the sound of his own squeaking voice, which being, however, first exerted in my service, may seem to have called for my gratitude. I had not been many minutes in the coach, when he exclaimed to some one who sat opposite to him, " My dear, you had better move your basket out of the gentleman's way, for I know there is nothing so uncomfortable as not

having room to stretch one's legs in, and my principle 's always to accommodate and be accommodated,—that's the way to shove on through life,—
nothing like it,—give a penny, and you'll often get
six-pence in return.   My love, put the basket on
your knee, and I'll carry that there *ridicil* for
you."   I turned to ascertain what individual of the
fair species was thus tenderly addressed, though I
had already discovered, to my cost, that she was,
in person at any rate, by no means an unsubstantial
dame.   In truth, I found that she completely made
up in her own form for the meagreness of him,
who I concluded to be her loving spouse, and she
appeared to consider that her superiority in size
ought to give her an undisputed ascendency in all
other things over her humble swain, whom she evidently held in the most sovereign contempt.   But
the poor little man, to do him justice, was not so
cowardly as to be in any way abashed or discon-
certed by her pettish exclamations or supercilious
nods, in spite of which he went chattering on,
without seeming to think it of any consequence
whether he was favoured with auditors or not.
Notwithstanding his loquacity, however, the admiral and I contrived to enter into a conversation,
which became gradually more and more interesting from the plain good sense by which it was distinguished on the part of my companion, and the

mass of general information which he possessed. Thus were two hours agreeably spent; the remarks and anecdotes with which the worthy admiral seasoned his discourse, being only occasionally interrupted by the questions, and the intended witticisms, of our facetious little fellow-passenger; as his better half, leaning back her head against the coach, and drawing her veilover her full rubicund features, resigned herself into the arms of Somnus. At length, the coach suddenly stopped, and, on looking out to ascertain the cause, I perceived a young woman, of the lower order, but respectably and modestly attired, standing by the side of the road, accompanied by another female, and evidently waiting to be taken up. She was leaning for support upon her companion, and her pale but interesting countenance, and fragile and half-bending form, seemed to bespeak her blessed with a very scanty portion of health. It had for some time looked black and lowering, and now the rain began heavily to descend. " Do you want an outside place, mistress?" called the coachman. " No," answered she, in an anxious and distressed tone, " I hope I can go inside." " The inside's full," he replied, " but you may get up behind," goodnaturedly adding, as the poor creature was every moment attacked by a painful cough, " as you don't seem to be well, I'll lend you this coat of mine to keep you dry." She thanked him for his offer, and was preparing to mount the coach, when her companion interposed, and warmly protested against her going on the outside; but, turning to her, with a look of bitter anguish, she said, " Oh! Mary! and if he were to go without my seeing him, do you think I could ever be happy again?" This answer appeared indisputable; and again she turned towards the coach, when the admiral springing from his seat, exclaimed, " 'Fore George! and I ride snugly here, while that poor maiden is shivering above me! No, by Neptune, I think," looking at himself, " I can brave many a good storm yet, but that poor lassie looks as if a gale of wind would shiver her in pieces. Here," said he, getting out, " Here is a warm birth for you inside, my pretty maiden, for, zounds! my legs are so confoundedly cramped, that I shall be glad to stretch them above deck there awhile," at the same time shaking first one and then the other, to convince her of the truth of his assertion. A half-murmured " God bless you, Sir," was all that she could utter in reply, as, accepting his offered arm, she took possession of his vacated seat; but the silent tear that trembled in her eyes spoke what her tongue refused to clothe in language. All had passed so quickly, that it was not till this instant, that, taking shame to myself for not having before

offered my place, (although I had but lately recovered from a dangerous illness, and was still called
an invalid,) I could start up, and insist upon the
admiral's accepting my empty corner. " No, no,
my good Sir," he replied, looking steadfastly at
me, " I suspect my old bones are tougher than
yours, and trust me, they will not injure by such a
scud of rain as this;" and so saying, he ascended
the roof, and my fair neighbour, nodding an
adieu to her companion, the coachman lashed his
horses, and again put us in motion, while the little
man opposite me, who had remained silent during
the whole of this scene, stammered forth something
like an apology for not having volunteered his
place; " But to tell you the truth, Sir," leaning
forward, and lowering his voice, while he commu-
nicated the important information, " I am terribly
subject to stiff necks, which you must own are very
disagreeable things,—very disagreeable indeed,—
and such a storm as this," shrugging up his
shoulders as he surveyed the prospect from the
window, " would certainly have given me one, as
sure as my name is Fulford." My new companion
did not seem inclined to utter a syllable, and, per-
ceiving that her thoughts were not fixed upon the
objects before her, I did not interrupt her reverie.
Several times her really pretty blue eyes filled
with tears, and she appeared to be struggling with

some inward emotion, but, at length, as if it had been entirely suppressed, her countenance, instead of the moving variations of grief, assumed the settled expression either of despair or of resignation. I longed to know what it was that afflicted her, though, had it been in my power to do so, nothing should have tempted me to gratify my curiosity at her expense. It seemed, however, that no delicate scruples assailed the self-complacent Mr. Fulford, who bluntly demanded, " Pray, my dear, are you going all the way to Portsmouth." The object to whom this inquiry was addressed started, as if suddenly roused to a recollection of where she was, but merely turning her head slightly towards the speaker, she gave a simple assent to his question. " Oh, oh! and may-be then, from what you said just now, you are going to see some relation off by the fleet that will sail to-morrow. Not your sweetheart, I hope, for that would be a bad job," at the same time peering slily in her face. This was too much. The string that grated so deeply at her heart had been touched with too rude a hand. All command was lost, and she burst into a flood of tears. " Nay," said the curious, but not I think ill-natured little man, who seemed really sorry for what he had done, " I am sure I did not intend to make you cry, but I couldn't guess you'd take on so." Anxious to stop his further commentaries, which I saw only increased her agitation, I gave him a significant nod, which, to my great joy, he seemed willing to comprehend. The poor girl gradually recovered her composure, and the rest of our journey was passed in almost total silence by the whole party.

At length we reached the place of our destination. The coach stopped, and porters, stable-boys, and chambermaids issued pell-mell out of the door of the inn at which we were to alight, while dirty boys and idle men assembled as usual round the gate-way, to see the vehicle stripped of all its loads, animate or inanimate. But only one form fixed the eye of the poor maiden within,— that of her sailor lover, who, with a fleet step, and a sparkling eye, approached to help her out. In a trice the door was opened, and she was by his side. "Oh! William—." " Fanny, dear Fanny," were the only words that I could catch ; but they were pronounced with the emphasis of deep as well as lively feeling, and they doubtless spoke more than volumes to the hearts to which they were respectively addressed. Tenderly wrapping the shawl that enveloped her more closely round his beloved, the young sailor gave her his arm, and was leading her away, when, catching a sight of the admiral, as he was bustling up to the spot where I stood, she turned towards him, and mo-

s

destly curtseying, thanked him for his kindness, and then hastily departed. "A happy meeting she has had," said the kind-hearted veteran, looking after her, "'twas a happy meeting, but I doubt if the poor thing will be carried far on the favourable gale of joy, for I suspect there's a heavy storm coming upon her, though it's only in consideration of her womanhood that I can forgive her grieving at giving up that fine young fellow to the service of his country. 'Fore George! I wish our navy was made up of such gallant-looking youngsters."

It was mutually agreed between my new friend and myself, that as we should both be temporary inhabitants of the inn at which we had alighted, we should spend the evening together; and we suited each other so well, that it was not until a very late hour that we separated.

The following morning early, we encountered each other again upon the beach, just as the last boat was waiting to convey those who were yet upon land to the fleet which was on the point of sailing. Persons of all descriptions were assembled on the spot, but it was easy to distinguish between those who were mere spectators of what was passing, and those who were themselves interested in the scene, and the tearful countenances,— the despairing looks of those who had recently parted with their friends, betrayed the " bitter tale." But there was one couple standing a little apart from the rest, who seemed unconscious of ought but their approaching separation. It was poor Fanny and her lover. At first, they appeared engaged in earnest conversation. Then, in this moment of deep emotion and high-wrought feeling, regardless of all that influences in the hour of cool reflection, I saw him snatch her to his breast, and imprint upon her cheek his parting kiss. He then essayed to tear himself away, but she clung to his arm with the pertinaceous grasp of affection, and it was not till he heard a summons for his departure, that he seemed to have courage to proceed. At last, they past together the place where I stood, and he turned to bid her one more long, final adieu. I heard him say, " Another kiss, dearest,—remember William!" " To my latest hour,—to my very grave,—but stop one moment,—only *one* moment. There was something—Oh! I remember," said she, taking from her bosom a little paper, containing, I doubted not, some token of affection, " look at this some time, when you are far away, and think of Fanny." " Come, young man," called a loud hoarse voice from the boat, " I can wait no longer." " Farewell, then, God for ever bless you!" was pronounced in low but emphatic words. At last, a fond embrace expressed the rest. In another instant he was in the boat. She stood for

some time motionless as a statue, in the spot where
he had left her; but when she saw her lover re-
ceding from the shore, and felt that he had indeed
left her, she rushed towards the waves, and holding out her arms, seemed by that mute act to
implore him to return to her. He could only wave
his hand. This parting signal opened the full tide
of sorrow. A flood of tears relieved her bursting
heart, and, retreating back a few yards, she remained with her eyes fixed upon the little bark
which contained her heart's dearest treasure. In a
short time, the fleet was in motion. The white
sails expanded by the wind bore the gallant vessels
swiftly along; and, as they cut through the swelling waves with their gay pennons floating in the
breeze, and their prows sparkling in the morning
sun, I felt that *this* was indeed a sight to raise
the proudest emotions in the breast of man, and
while he surveys these his own mighty works, to
make him forget for an instant how weak and frail
a creature he really is. But as in the moral world
distance (in time) often clears away the mists of
prejudice, and enables us to attain more nearly
the medium of truth, so in the present case distance (in space) soon showed me the folly of all
human vanity, and when I saw *that* fleet which so
lately had astonished and even awed me by its
grandeur, gradually dwindling away, until it was

scarcely to be distinguished from the blue line of the horizon, I became aware of how vast is the chasm which separates the works of man, and those of his Creator, and how really and intrinsically insignificant are the most splendid monuments of human power.

The crowd which had been collected together now began to disperse. Many of those who composed it hastened away; others formed themselves into small parties to pass the time in trivial conversation, while some of the sea-faring men resumed their usual occupations as if nothing had happened to interrupt them. But there was *one* who heard not, saw not, any thing that was passing around her. The desolate Fanny, as if rooted to the earth, continued to gaze upon that solitary speck which still glistened afar off upon the ocean. The advancing waves rolled over her feet; she felt—she heeded them not. A rough tar spoke to her as he passed, but his voice was to her but as the wind; and it was not until she could descry nothing save a vast and fathomless expanse of waters, that, as if awakened to a full sense of her deprivation, she clasped her hands together, muttered some piteous exclamation, and then moved slowly towards the town, turning, however, every moment, to take another glance at the quarter in which the fleet had disappeared from her sight. I also turned, and, by this movement, became sensible that my friend the admiral was still standing by my side. His eyes yet glistened with tears,—his lip yet trembled with emotion. "Poor thing! poor thing!" he ejaculated with a subdued voice; and then, as if ashamed of his weakness, dashing away the soft drop of pity as it rolled unbidden down his cheek, he exclaimed, "I did not think I was such an old fool! I, that have seen my own father drop down dead by my side, and felt bullets whizzing round my head by dozens, to be playing the woman, and at the sight of a love-sick girl too!" "My dear Sir," said I, my heart responding too faithfully to his, and a glow of enthusiasm pervading my breast, "Pure is the source, and ever sacred be the tear of humanity—Let it flow. 'Tis the glistening emanation of virtue,—the voluntary tribute of tender feeling,—the beautiful emblem of compassionate sympathy with the woes of others. 'Tis the bright drop that honours and exalts the man, and almost deifies the Christian!"

Eight years! Is it possible? Yes, eight *long* years after the little incident which I have been relating had taken place, I was wandering with a friend through a pretty village in the south of England. We had passed the church, with its sombre row of clipped yew-trees planted round it; the little parsonage which stood on one side, and

the old grey farm-house which occupied the ground
on the other; and had arrived at a green knoll,
on which stood two little neat cottages, as well as
one of larger dimensions, and which was dignified
by the addition of an old-fashioned porch, in which
doubtless many a tale had been told, in days of old,
by the village gossips. About the distance of ten
yards from this, and in the middle of the little
green, was placed " *in terrorem*," that dread of
many a roguish lad, the stocks, which, however, in
the present instance, seemed to be divested of all
its usual horrors, by two perpendicular sticks which
were fastened upon it, to support another in a
horizontal position, the whole apparently intended
to form an instrument for the learned game of
leap-frog. That it was really meant to answer this
purpose was speedily exemplified by a crowd of
urchins who issued from the aforesaid porch in
riotous confusion; and then, as if under one common impulse, ran after each other to this object
of attraction, and sprang nimbly over it. After
this feat had been several times performed, and the
boys were settling, with vociferous eagerness, the
important point of what sport they should next
pursue, a young man of very respectable appearance, but who, I perceived, had had one of his
legs supplied with a wooden one, came from the
cottage, (or rather, perhaps, I ought to honour it

with the title of house,) and calling to one of his youngest boys, he desired him to leave his companions for awhile, as his mother wanted him within. Having for some time been wishing to meet with a person who could give us information respecting the village which we were desirous to obtain, we hastened to the young man who was still standing by the door, and who received us with a respectful bow, answered our queries, and civilly requested us to walk in, and rest ourselves. While he was speaking, something in his whole appearance gave me an indistinct idea of my having seen him before, and, as this feeling strengthened with every passing moment, I readily accepted his offer, thinking that I might perhaps be able to recall to my mind when we could have met. We accordingly entered a small but beautifully neat apartment, out of which an open door disclosed a much larger room, where scattered books and benches declared the purpose to which it was dedicated. We found a pleasing-looking woman nursing a sweet infant, and the little curly-headed boy I had just seen without, standing by her side, with his face turned up towards hers with an expression of the most earnest attention. She rose, while a slight blush passed over her cheek at our unexpected entrance, and requested us to be seated, a luxury which we really enjoyed, after a long and fatiguing walk. I thought my fancy must surely be cheating me with chimeras, as, on again looking at the female before me, I conceived she also was not an entire stranger to me, and I was puzzling my brain to account for what I imagined to be merely some strange coincidence, when I perceived her regarding me with fixed and silent attention. At this instant, the real truth flashed on my memory. It was the Fanny who had so strongly excited my commiseration at Portsmouth, whom I beheld, divested indeed of the pallid hue of sickness, which was supplied by the soft bloom of health; and with this reminiscence before me, on looking again at the young man who was now standing by her, I did not fail to recognise in his good-humoured face and manly form, mutilated as it was, the *William* of her choice.

This discovery greatly delighted me, for I had long sought in vain for some clue by which I might ascertain the residence of my friend the admiral, or whether indeed he still held a place among the living; and I immediately made myself known, and congratulated the fortunate Fanny on the happy termination of her sorrows. "Ah! Sir," replied she, after the first natural expressions of wonder and surprise had been involuntarily uttered, "Ah! Sir, but if it had not been for that blessed gentleman who, you may remember, got out of the coach in pity to me, I should never have been here to tell my happy lot;" at the same time glancing up to her husband with a look of artless affection which needed no interpreter.

Made eloquent by the inspiring emotions of gratitude, she then recounted to me all that he had done for her, which, with a narration I afterwards received from her spouse, I will condense into a few words, for the edification of my readers.

It seemed that when I first met with Fanny, she was living with an aged mother, who had been reduced from a comparatively comfortable situation into one of extreme poverty, and whom she supported by means of such unremitting industry as proved fatal to her health. The tenderness and attention of her lover, however, whose home was near her own, soothed and supported her, and at last she had consented to his earnest wishes of a speedy union, when her mother was seized with an illness which threatened to terminate her existence, and then every thing else was forgotten in her anxiety for this cherished object of her care. At last her duteous attention was rewarded by the partial revival of her parent; but she escaped one misfortune only to endure the anguish inflicted by another. Just at this time, her lover was summoned to the post of duty. Aware of the injurious effects which a parting interview might have upon the delicate health of his betrothed, he courageously departed without bidding her adieu, leaving, however, behind him an epistle fraught with expressions of never-ending affection, and cheered with hopes of better days and brighter prospects. But though he thus essayed to soften it, the blow fell most heavily. " I will see him once again," said she, " I will take a last farewell." She inquired when the fleet would sail, despatched a few hasty lines to her lover to entreat him to remain until the last moment on shore, and then set off with the melancholy determination of bidding him " good bye," for ever.

But from this dark moment her story gradually brightens. After I left Portsmouth, the good admiral made inquiries of her situation, discovered her abode, and unknown to her, sent her a skilful physician, by whose aid and attention she was in a few months restored to comparative health. Her poor mother, however, was past all human assistance, and worn out by disease and age, she expired, while, through the means of this same physician, with whom it was afterwards discovered he held a constant correspondence, the admiral defrayed the expenses of her humble funeral, and settled an annual stipend upon the afflicted daughter. On this, and the money she procured by her own labour, the poor desolate maiden lived by herself, in the cottage which had once been gladdened by the fond smile of a parent, and the tender voice of a lover. She was one evening sitting by her door, with the work by which she maintained herself upon her knee; the sun's last parting beams had disappeared, and the shades of evening were gathering thickly around; all nature was hushed, and no sound was heard save now and then the solitary note of some little bird which was not yet gone to its mossy couch. The scene well accorded with the feelings of the lovely mourner; she sat gazing intently upon the dark blue sky, but thinking of the days that were gone, and re-calling with a sort of melancholy satisfaction, the looks and the actions of the cold tenant of the grave, and the wanderer of the ocean. Suddenly, the latch of the little gate by her side was lifted up—she turned almost unconsciously at the sound—a low voice murmured the name of " Fanny !"—she started, she rushed forward,—she fainted upon the breast of her lover !

I need add little more to this simple tale. Suffice that the poor fellow had lost a leg in the service of his country, and that a pension was therefore settled upon him for life, and he was discharged from the service. He married his adored Fanny, rendered still dearer to him than ever by the sorrows and the sufferings she had undergone. And the admiral hearing of the event, visited himself the happy couple, and offered the husband the situation of schoolmaster in the village of ——— ———. As he had received a tolerable education, he accepted it with thankfulness; and the sight of the happiness of this deserving pair must no doubt have afforded to him who caused it a reward the sweetest, the most delightful, that it was possible for him to receive.

Finding, upon further inquiry, that the admiral resided at a very short distance from the village, I set out the following morning to pay him a visit. On applying for admission at the door of a large substantial-looking mansion, surrounded by gardens and pleasure-grounds, laid out after the usual English fashion, I was ushered into a room where I found the veteran, who had braved the perils of the sea, and passed safely through the toil and the dangers of many a " hard-fought " battle, fastened down to a large easy chair, in the chimney-corner, by that arch enemy, the gout, the sharp twinges of which he could neither "fly nor defy." However, they did not appear to have soured his temper, or put his benevolence to flight, for he was playing off sundry tricks and antics for the amusement of a little girl, whom I afterwards found to be his favourite grand-daughter, and who was rolling on

the carpet before him, in convulsions of laughter.
Three fine-looking young women (his daughters)
were also in the room, besides the wife of his eldest
son, who was staying at his house. When he
heard my name announced, the old man, forgetting
his gout, half started from his seat, till painfully
reminded of it by the movement, he sunk down
again, and contented himself with cordially holding out his hand, at the same time exclaiming,
" To think of this cursed gout tying me here,
when a friend is heaving-to in my own port. Why,
my good friend, I thought fate had decreed we
should not meet any more on the ocean of life, but
a favourable gale has wafted you here at last, and,
by the Majesty of Neptune! it shall be an evil one
that carries you away again." After being introduced to the rest of the party, we naturally re-
verted to the last and only time we had so agreeably
passed together. " Well, our poor maiden is safely
and snugly lodged in the harbour of wedlock," said
the admiral ; " the young tar came back with one
of his main supporters lopt off, so he was obliged
to lie-to for the rest of his life, and he could not do
better, you know, than get the pretty lassie to keep
him company." " Yes," I replied emphatically,
" I saw them yesterday, and heard them bless the
benevolent friend who had procured for them the

happiness which they enjoy, and enjoy gratefully."
" Oh—Oh," stammered he, " you have seen them,
then, have you ?" and immediately he quitted the
subject, evidently desirous that it should be no
more enlarged upon. His was, indeed, that true
Christian charity which " vaunteth not itself," and
is not " puffed up," but which, flowing on in one
mild and gentle current, fertilized and gladdened
every region through which it passed.

I found that I was, in truth, what my old friend
declared, " securely harboured," for I found it
impossible to quit the agreeable circle which I had
entered, until a late hour in the evening, nor could
I then succeed in making good my retreat, without promising to repeat my visit.

This day was the commencement of an inter-
course which has afforded me many sources of
heartfelt pleasure, and I shall never fail to bless
that Providence which so graciously added to my
stock of real and valued friends.

The good admiral is now very old ; but still
cheerful, still loving and beloved, he delights in
telling stories of his younger days, in relating to
his grand-children the history of battles and of
sieges, in once more acting in imagination the hero
and the British tar, and exulting again in the triumphs of his country ; and when he goes down to

the silent grave, he will be followed by the blessings and the regrets of many, and the love of all
to whom he is known.   Like the majestic tree of
the forest, he may be cut off from the earth, but
his place will long be remembered with veneration,
and recognised with melancholy joy.

———

THE POET'S HOUR.

The mind of man, inconstant as it is, bears the strong impress of the creative hand of its great and wise Designer.

Of the many proofs which are daily crowding around us, of the mutability of every thing within our sphere of knowledge, none is more striking than that presented by the human mind, which is subject to constant variation, and always liable to be acted upon by outward causes. Like the thermometer, it is continually rising or falling, as the atmosphere of life becomes in the slightest degree rarer or more dense, and thus elevates or depresses those powerful agents, the feelings. Sometimes, indeed, it will be brightly illuminated, or fearfully overcast, without any apparent reason, either for the pleasing sun shine, or the threatening cloud, and a few hours will witness the same mind possessed by the cheering influence of hope, or subdued by the evil demon despair. That, which by the aid of its natural formation, assisted by firm and steady principles, preserves the most even

T

balance between these extremes, amongst the fluctuations of the world, is indisputably the happiest; but even such an one will, like a fine but delicate instrument of music, be liable to be jarred by a thousand unforeseen accidents; and to be sometimes deprived of its sweetest tones by even a touch upon some of its susceptible notes and wires.

Though this liability of the human mind to be influenced by the most trifling circumstances, may be sometimes productive of temporary pain, it is yet very frequently the source of much mental enjoyment, and affords us moments of delight which we should not experience were we at all times equally affected by the pleasures which surround us. For instance, what power does Nature possess at some seasons over our feelings! and how do her beautiful and varied scenes swell the glow of rapture, or wake the throb of enthusiastic joy in our breasts! What delight will she sometimes diffuse through hearts, before perhaps sunk into useless despondency! and what unaccountable transitions will she unconsciously produce from sorrow and discontent, to happiness and peace! Thus, a sweet summer's evening, when all is still and silent, and a soothing calm seems spread every where around, will not fail to harmonize a susceptible mind to its own state of happy placidity; or a fine clear morning to raise in it emotions of a livelier but not a less pleasurable nature. It is surely a very merciful provision of the Almighty so to constitute us, that we may be open to such innocent gratifications as these; and to him, therefore, ought we to dedicate those pleasing thoughts which, by his goodness, were first graciously created.

It was on such a morning as I describe, when the verdure of spring was succeeding the desolation of winter, and when all nature seemed to joy in the renovation of its long-concealed beauties, that, inspired by sentiments of the purest love and gratitude to the great Being who had thus clothed the world with loveliness, and formed man with a mind capable of appreciating its enjoyments, I poured out my soul with humble reverence to Him, in the following lines, endeavouring to utter, (although most feebly,) the grateful sense I entertained of the blessings so lavishly bestowed on frail mortality, and entreating that, by his wondrous power, he would make me more worthy and deserving of them. As all have abundant cause for thankfulness, and (though perhaps less sinful,) are still but " weak children of the dust," both the praises and the supplications must be to all more or less applicable. I will, therefore, make no apology for inserting them here, only observing, that I claim nothing for them but the merit of sincerity, for of

what else can a poor finite mortal boast, when ad
dressing Infinite Perfection?—

> Oh Lord, my God! omnipotent and wise,
> To thee I raise my supplicating eyes;
> To thee, with grateful heart, I bend my knee,
> And in meek accents raise a prayer to Thee!—
> Now, Oh my Father! when all Nature's dawn
> Proclaims the opening of another morn;
> When the blest sun, in radiant glory bright,
> Dispels the solemn stillness of the night;
> When renovated nature smiles in joy,
> And owns a God, who made not to destroy;
> When ev'ry beast and bird combine to raise
> Their various notes of gratitude and praise;
> I too, with voice sincere, though numbers weak,
> The mix'd emotions of my soul would speak;
> I, too, my heart's best feelings would declare,
> And tell the humble love I cherish there.
>
> Oh Thou! whose bounteous spirit breathes around,
> By all is felt,—through all the earth is found;
> Whom neither ear hath heard, nor eye can see,
> Enshrin'd in solemn, sacred mystery;
> Who reign'st in glorious majesty above,
> Known but in mercy, seen alone in love;
> Pure is this breath of morn, but purer still
> The heart that bends submissive to thy will;
> Sweet is this scene,—for, Oh! whate'er I see
> Speaks to my soul of holiness and Thee.
> It tells me, that, though sinful, frail, and weak,
> I yet may dare my *gratitude* to speak;

That, though my heart has bow'd at Mammon's shrine,
It still, *in penitence*, may sue at thine ;
That, (Oh ! transcendent Mercy !) thou wilt hear,
And, hearing, grant a trembling suppliant's prayer.
That prayer, O God, will contrite strains prefer,
It begs for pardon, but it begs with *fear* ;
It sues for strength to follow and embrace
The purest doctrines of thy boundless grace.

Give me a spirit form'd in virtue's mould,
Itself distrusting, for religion bold ;
Pure as the zephyrs that around me blow,
Desiring, longing, all thy truth to know ;
Waiting in hope the bright, the blissful day,
That breaks its fetters with this form of clay ;
A heart with piety and kindness warm'd,
By pity soften'd, and by goodness charm'd ;
Illumined by the Sun of truth and light,
Whose ray's its beacon,—pure, unfading, bright.
—A mind unmoved by sorrow's ruthless blast,
Believing, hoping, trusting to the last ;
Bending submissive to thy chast'ning rod,
While praising all thy goodness, O my God !
Firm and unshaken 'midst temptation's lure,
Strong to oppose, though patient to endure ;
And if prosperity's enlivening ray
Shall gild the progress of my earthly way,
If in my path be strew'd life's choicest flowers,
And joy and pleasure mark the passing hours,—
On Thee—my Father, may it still rely,
Still dread the glance of thine all-piercing eye ;
May neither pride corrupt, nor vice ensnare,
Nor vain conceit e'er reign ungovern'd there.

And when, my God, my Father, and my Friend,
My fleeting days approach their destined end,—
When earth and all its scenes shall fade away
Before the prospect of eternal day,—
When all its joys recede before my sight,
Then fix'd on regions of unchanging light,—
Oh ! gently stay at last my passing breath,
And lead me calmly through the gates of death ;
Then bid my 'raptured spirit soar on high,
To sing Hosannahs in its native sky ;
To tune on golden harps its Maker's praise,
And songs of grateful love incessant raise.

LONDON:
Printed by WILLIAM CLOWES,
Northumberland court.

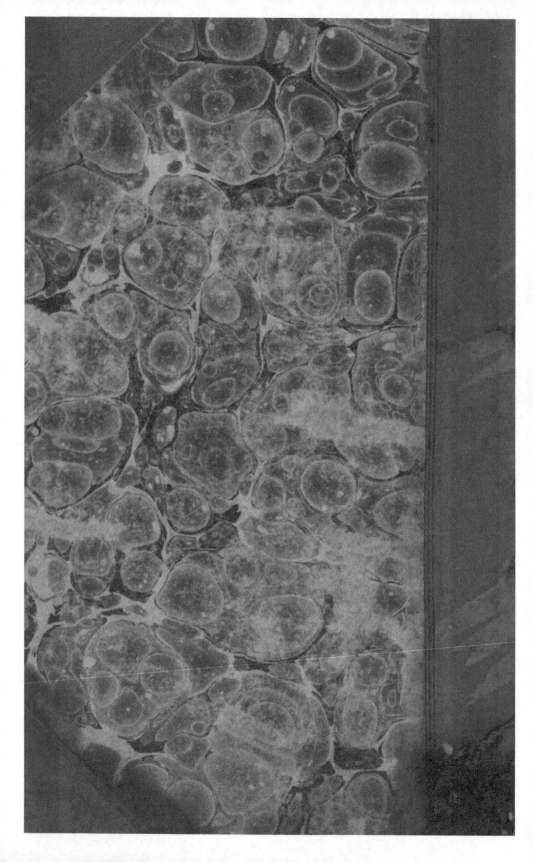

Check Out More Titles From HardPress Classics Series In this collection we are offering thousands of classic and hard to find books. This series spans a vast array of subjects — so you are bound to find something of interest to enjoy reading and learning about.

Subjects:
Architecture
Art
Biography & Autobiography
Body, Mind &Spirit
Children & Young Adult
Dramas
Education
Fiction
History
Language Arts & Disciplines
Law
Literary Collections
Music
Poetry
Psychology
Science
…and many more.

Visit us at www.hardpress.net

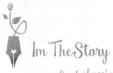

CPSIA information can be obtained
at www.ICGtesting.com
Printed in the USA
BVHW091901220819
556561BV00021B/5020/P

9 781318 527090